In Spite of Me...
Learning to Hear and Obey God's Voice

Cordula Dombrowsky

All Scriptures are from the New International Version of the Bible.
Copyright © 1973, 1978, 1984 by International Bible Society
Published by Hodder and Stoughton

Layout and cover : Dwight Hutchison

DEDICATION

This book is dedicated to all the wonderful people who, over the course of the years, have stood by me as I undertook this wild journey of walking by faith, of obeying the call into full-time missions.

You have believed in me, encouraged me, supported me, prayed for me. Your faithfulness, your friendship, your partnership has been invaluable!

May this book be a reminder of what you have invested into God's kingdom!

"Your name and your renown
are the desire of my heart."
Isaiah 26:8b

FOREWORD

"I have been privileged to know Cordula for over 25 years, but then again I feel like I have just met her in the pages of this short book. As I read through each entry I found myself laughing, crying, but always being challenged with my own walk with Christ. This is a book I just could not put down!

Cordula has always been one of my personal "heroes". I have watched her go through many of the trials of life, but each time she comes out looking a little more like Christ. I can only pray I can follow her example in my own life.

Her call to missions has been tested, yet her commitment has only been strengthened. I have often shared her story in the different teaching venues I am privileged to speak in. It is a modern day life story which impacts many who hear it. So often we all become discouraged and want to walk away from God's calling on our lives. Cordula's story is one that encourages all of us to remain faithful despite life's ups and downs.

This is a book I will give to many as they pursue their personal walk with the Lord. Thank you, Cordula, for sharing a little bit of your life and missions experiences with us. The rest we will have to wait and hear when we are with you in His Kingdom."

*Art J. Collins, former pastor, now a much loved
YWAM speaker and Bible teacher.*

ACKNOWLEDGEMENTS

A very special thank you to Maria Gilbertson, friend and coach, who spurred me on, week by week, giving advice and encouraging me to keep going. I doubt that I would have finished this book project without you!

Daniel Schaerer, who was the first to encourage me to write. Dwight Hutchison, for his gracious help with the layout and cover page. Tom and Linda P, who spent hours editing and giving precious advice. Karen P, Linda U, Norm W, who took the time to read through the manuscript. Thank you for your comments and suggestions!

Pastor Patrick M, who through a word of prophecy gave me the final confirmation to step out in faith and write.

Most of all, I thank the Lord for laying this book project on my heart, for giving me the courage and the energy to pursue it, for providing a safe place for me to write, and for believing in me.

Thank you!

TABLE OF CONTENTS

INTRODUCTION

It all started with this little story, "Precious Product."

Upon a sudden impulse, I sat down and wrote it. Within minutes my little story was on paper. I wondered where the inspiration had come from. The story was true, of course. All my stories are true, but this time my writing style was so different.

A few weeks later, another inspiration, another story.

Then I had the distinct feeling that God was calling me to write a book. I waited for quite some time as I was not convinced that I had the ability to write. But suddenly people started challenging me to do it. So here it is, the final outcome.

My prayer is that you will be challenged and encouraged throughout the pages of this book. And even though most of my stories are missions related, what I have experienced is valid for every Christian, whether you are a businessman, a college student or a stay-at-home parent. God speaks to each one of us in the same way.

And if you do not believe in God, it does not matter because God believes in you. So I hope that you too will be encouraged.

Different people are mentioned in this book. To protect their privacy, only first names are used and even those are mostly changed.

1

OF COURSE, YOU CAN!

I was back again in the little village high up in the mountains. As soon as I arrived the women gathered around me in
their brightly coloured dresses. What a joy to see them again!
The language barrier prevented in-depth communication, but
not affection. The smiles, the hugs needed no language. Most
of the women up in that poor area were uneducated.

The men, however, all spoke French. The leaders of the little
church greeted me warmly. We were in a Muslim nation, but
there were small groups of Christians in many villages and
towns. A revival was taking place.

"The women are so happy to see you again. They are looking
forward to the seminar."

"What seminar?" We were eating. I was munching away,
happily looking around. How I loved this place.

"The three day seminar you will be holding. You will be
teaching every morning, afternoon and evening."

"What? I cannot do that." I was totally unprepared. I had
taught there previously, but never a full seminar. But then, of
course, they could not have informed me. The phones did not
connect so high up, nor was there internet. And for security
reasons, they could not have communicated anyway.

"You must. The women have been praying and fasting for a week. They are so excited."

I was aghast. I could never do that. There was no time to prepare.

The leaders grinned and laughed. "Of course, you can! The Holy Spirit will help you."

He did. He helped me. I got a crash course in listening to the Holy Spirit and learnt to prepare messages in less than 15 minutes. To my surprise, the women would exclaim: "You chose the very subject we had been fasting and praying for."

I was still happy though, when the seminar was over. It had been a challenge. So I was thankful when a visiting pastor came and whisked me off to another village. Up, up into the mountains. We walked for a long time. Cars could not make it up here. Finally, we reached a small village and entered a courtyard. The women were outside, cooking. We were invited to sit in a room which contained only one weak light bulb. Soon it was dark. In the dim light, I saw others join us until the little room was packed. We huddled together as we ate. I was happy. It was so nice to just relax now. I wondered what would happen next. Suddenly the pastor nudged me. "It will be your turn in a few minutes." "Turn for what?" "To preach."

I dropped my plate and hurriedly picked up my Bible. I had five minutes to prepare a message. I was in a different world. The world of oral people who do not write notes when preparing a message.

2

I AM A TCK

Oh, but before I continue, I must tell you that I am a TCK (a Third-Culture Kid).

TCKs are children whose parents have settled into a nation that is not their own. TCKs, therefore, grow up in a land that differs from the culture, social, religious and language background of their parents' homeland. TCKs are generally children of diplomats, expats, missionaries, or refugees.

TCKs become experts in weaving in and out of their various cultures. In the home, they adjust to the culture of their parents, who generally maintain their own culture despite the geographical move they have made. Outside of the home, TCKs adopt the culture of the land they are living in. They also quite naturally make a mix of both cultures, producing a third culture. Hence the term, *third-culture kids.* This learning experience enables them in later years to move in and out of multiple cultures, adapting to the people-groups around them with much ease. It is a tremendous advantage.

But when you're in a mission organisation like mine, you often attend international conferences. At one point or another, someone feels obligated to ask people to stand up according to where they are from. This is when you're not sure where you are from and you spend the rest of the evening wondering about it. Your mind wanders off as you re-evaluate your roots. The rest of the evening becomes a blur. What was this conference about anyway?

When TCKs leave their adopted homeland to return to their parents' native country, this is the one place in the world that presents the biggest challenges for them, due to a deep sense of loss. The loss of roots, friends, belongings, familiar smells, sounds, sights, and tastes. Childhood memories are plugged into the adopted nation that has become their *home,* but not the country of their origin. Others assume that they are rejoicing by being in the country of their nationality, yet they themselves do not feel *at home.* This uprooted feeling can be devastating. The grieving process is long because there are so many losses to deal with at the same time.

An uprooting is intensified for TCKs because the *return* to their parents' country is not really a return at all. Their parents return, but for TCKs, it is an *arrival* into a new setting.

I was born in Namibia. My parents were from Germany. We moved on to South Africa and then to the beautiful island of Mauritius. When I was eighteen, we were uprooted. My father had died suddenly. We had to leave our sweet island home. I arrived in Berlin, Germany in January. It was winter. It was snowing and cold. I came from an isle that knew no snow, no winter.

It took me years to overcome this sense of loss. The constant drive to re-plant my roots. Somewhere. Somehow.

If you are a TCK and are still grappling with a loss of roots, my best advice to you is to revisit the country of your birth, your childhood years. Go back and walk around. Smell, see, and taste. It will bring healing to your soul. A return to your roots is crucial. It will bring closure to the past and enable you to envision the future. It happened to me. Believe me, it helps.

3

A RESTLESS NOMAD

"A horse?"

We had met in Hamburg, Germany. He was a successful lawyer. When he had first picked me up in his shiny Mercedes Benz sports car, my girlfriend had groaned with envy. Not sure whether it was his car or his looks. Probably both. Ever so often we would spend weekends on his sail boat. But after a year, it didn't look like he was considering a lifelong relationship. So, I left. I did not like Hamburg anyway. Nor had I liked Berlin. Nothing compared to my island, Mauritius.

Somehow I made it to Brussels. But a year later he had found me there and pleaded for me to return. Except that now I wasn't sure anymore. I didn't even like sailing, not in the North Sea. Too cold for an island girl. Until he mentioned the horse. He offered to buy me one. Now that got me thinking. You see, I love horses. But somehow it didn't seem right. So I wished him farewell, the rich and handsome lawyer.

I returned to my little 10 square meter apartment. I had no money, no job and, of course, no horse.

My father's sudden death earlier on had drowned all my prospects of studying. So it had been job-hunting instead. I eventually found a position as a secretary and a nicer apartment. But I was still restless, a nomad searching for a home. At that point, a traveling businessman invited me to work for him in Vienna, Austria. Apart from the fact that he was an associate of my employer in Brussels, I did not really know him, but it seemed the right thing to do. So I packed my bags... again. I was twenty-one years old.

I settled into my new surroundings in Vienna and started doing office work for my new employer. He was the CEO of a flourishing business. I wondered why he had recruited me. I made lots of mistakes, but he did not seem to care.

After about a week, he invited me to travel with him to the beautiful city of Salzburg. It was to be an important business meeting and he needed my (not so perfect) secretarial skills. We had a pleasant drive down from Vienna. To my surprise, he parked the car in front of the famous five-star hotel, the *Goldener Hirsch.*

We dined in the hotel's exquisite restaurant. The food was delicious. We were waited on like a king and queen. I wondered when the business meeting would take place.

Eventually we wandered off to the royal suite he had booked. I was about to go into my little side bedroom, when, to my utmost surprise, he knelt down and asked me to marry him! I was stunned. I hardly knew him. He was so much older than me. Well, at least 10 years older. I said "No." And I was fired.

I guess I should have said: "Let me think about this one." But I didn't.

4

IAEA, VIENNA

I found no other job. Without diplomas, things were difficult. Until I saw this bulletin from the United Nations. They were recruiting English speaking office staff. I doubted that they would accept me, but I had run out of other options. I applied and was invited to come for an interview. It was December, cold and snowy. I walked into the office of the personnel manager, a sweet middle-aged lady. As soon as she saw me, she exclaimed: "My dear, is that the only coat you have?"

It was. Indeed, it was not really suited for such a cold wintry day. And, no, I did not have the means to afford a more suitable coat. She was aghast. She started flipping through her papers. She really wanted to find me a job, but it was hard because I had no degrees and so little experience. In desperation, she asked me if I spoke any other languages. I told her that I spoke German and French as well as the English we were communicating in. She immediately called in a mother tongue French speaker and also a German speaker. The verdict fell. Both confirmed that I spoke fluently. I found out that I had three mother tongues. Not that I cared, but dear Teresa was delighted. She had found me a job.

Her compassionate heart had opened up a door of hope for

me. I started work as a secretary for the United Nations at the IAEA (International Atomic Energy Agency). The work there was pleasant. People were friendly and polite. I developed friendships with co-workers and we would go out partying and eating out in fancy restaurants.

Oh, and then there were the various amenities on the UN compound (restaurants, travel agency, duty free shop, to name only a few.)

And, last but not least, a very generous salary.

I slowly climbed up the career ladder until that day which radically changed my life.

5

THE ENCOUNTER

I woke up with a start. This dream, again. I did not like it. Somehow it seemed real, and it made me feel guilty. I realised that I had hurt someone. Suddenly I felt uncomfortable. I had no idea what *conviction of sin* was. I did not believe in God.

Then I had this distinct feeling that *someone* was watching me from above. Who was it?

I asked my friends. But they were atheists, just like me, and had no explanation to offer.

Then one night I had a different dream in which a former friend from school invited me to come to Mauritius for a visit. I instinctively felt that I needed to do just that. So I bought an airline ticket and flew off. I sensed I was going to find the answer there.

Upon my arrival, my former fun-loving, beach party friends in Mauritius told me that they wanted to introduce me to someone who I was sure to love. His name was Jesus. I was stunned. They had become Christians. Their eyes were beaming. It was obvious that they had some wild encounter.

So there I was, trapped on this island, listening to my crazy friends. What they said didn't seem to line up intellectually, but the more they talked, the more I sensed that this was the truth.

Before flying back home, they gave me a book entitled *World Aflame* written by Billy Graham. Reading a spiritual book wasn't really on my agenda. I wanted a restful flight. Once on board, I fumbled around in my handbag trying to find another book I had bought, but I mistakenly pulled out Billy Graham's book. So I figured I could at least skim through the introductory page. That first page caught my attention. I spent the rest of the 15-hour flight back to Vienna reading. I was spellbound. I finished the book and by the time I got home, everything was clear in my mind. I knew what I wanted.

My wise friends had also given me a cassette (that's a 20th-century recording tape) and on it, someone preached. At the end of his message, the preacher invited people to repeat his prayer. I knew I had to do just that. As I prayed, the whole room and my whole life swerved. Jesus had stepped into the room. I felt His presence. I saw Him, not clearly, but as in a blur. A weight of burdens was lifted off me. As these burdens left, I felt waves of love overwhelm me. I knew at that moment that Jesus loved me... I was forgiven and that it was for all eternity. I wept for several hours without stopping. The emptiness in my heart was filled to overflowing.

6

BAPTISM

The next day, a thought that seemed almost like an audible voice flashed through my mind: "Go and get baptised." I remembered my parents telling me about Baptists. I knew Baptists baptise. That's why they are called Baptists. So, I looked for a Baptist church and went there the following Sunday. The church service was wonderful. Right after, I went to see the pastor and asked him to baptise me, but he wanted to know who I was and I had to tell him all about how I met Jesus. I didn't understand why he wanted all that information. All I wanted was to get baptised.

The pastor was really friendly. He invited me to come back and share my story with the elders of his church. One of them said that it wasn't possible to meet Jesus without having read the Bible first. That really confused me, but the pastor told the man that I had experienced a charismatic conversion. I didn't know what that meant. All I wanted was to get baptised.

Well, I finally did get baptised. It took several weeks, but I made it into the baptismal pond. I was overjoyed.

At that time I also got really excited about the Bible. I read the first Gospel, then the second one, the third one and the fourth Gospel. And then I searched for the fifth Gospel, but

I couldn't find it. I was very disappointed because I wanted more stories about Jesus. So I reread the four Gospels and eventually started reading the Acts of the Apostles.

What I read about the Holy Spirit stirred my heart and I asked the people in my church about him. They said I already had the Holy Spirit. But I felt I was missing something. So, I decided to fly to Israel, because I figured if that's where Jesus had lived, then the Holy Spirit must surely be there. A girlfriend decided to come along. She was interested in Buddhism at that time. She was very kind and kept asking: "Have you found him yet?" But I didn't, even though we went to lots of places in Israel. I flew back to Vienna feeling very discouraged.

7

THE CALLING

In desperation, I wrote to my Mauritian friends who had since moved to South Africa. I asked them where I could find the Holy Spirit and they told me to come to South Africa. So I bought an airline ticket and flew to Johannesburg.

My friends prayed for me all night long, but nothing happened. But three days later, these strange and beautiful words came out of my mouth. It was very unexpected and very unusual. I had received the gift of praying in tongues. I was delighted.

Not long afterwards, something amazing happened. I heard these clear, almost audible words: "I want you to leave your job. I am calling you to missions." I was stunned. I knew it was God. But why me? Somehow I felt I couldn't say *no,* so I said yes and then a wave of joy flooded all over me. That's when I learnt that it's always best to say yes to God.

I went back to Vienna and told my boss at the IAEA that I was resigning in order to become a missionary. He was very surprised. In fact, everybody was surprised. I didn't know where I was meant to go to be a missionary, but I resigned anyway. The personnel director, dear Teresa, heard about my planned departure and came to see me. She offered me a golden opportunity to move up the ladder in my career. But, even as she spoke, I just knew that I had to decline her offer. God had told me to become a missionary.

I still had several months at the UN and while I was waiting to know what to do, I heard about a Bible study group within the UN complex. I decided to join them. I had so much to learn from the Bible. I was still a baby Christian. I loved every minute of that first meeting. In the end, the leader came up to me and asked me to take over leadership of the Bible Study from that time on. I couldn't believe what she said. I knew nothing. But she was insistent. I had the gift, the anointing, she said. So I led the study group. I struggled, but I did. I don't know how, but I managed to lead a group of older and more mature Christians until my departure from the UN.

And somehow I even organised an official evangelistic campaign in the chapel of the UN headquarters. But that was after I had heard about YWAM.

8

YWAM

One day I visited a church where I met a group from a missions organisation called YWAM. I was so amazed by what they said. They talked about God like they really knew Him well. I asked if I could come and visit them and the next weekend I was at their base. It was an old hotel in the mountains near Vienna, a beautiful place. I spent the weekend there and on the Sunday before leaving, I asked if I could join them.

"Yes, you can come. We have prayed about you and know that you have a clear call to missions. You can join us now and eventually attend our Discipleship Training School (DTS)."

I had no idea what a DTS was. It sounded like some sort of biblical training, and that was exactly what I wanted.

A month before I moved to join the YWAM base outside of Vienna, a Christian friend asked me what I was going to do about financial support. I didn't understand. I told him that it didn't matter if I just got a small salary, like just board and lodging, plus a little pocket-money. He informed me that YWAM didn't do that and that I needed to learn to *live by faith.* I didn't know what that meant, but for some strange reason, I didn't care. I was so happy to become a missionary. Besides, I had plenty of money on my account. It was enough to pay for the Discipleship Training School and more.

In the meantime, almost everyone around me thought I had gone insane and tried to dissuade me. My boss was particularly concerned and even went all the way to check out the YWAM base. But I knew that this was where God wanted me to go.

Soon I handed in the keys to my beautiful rental apartment. It was located in one of the fancy areas in Vienna. I had treated myself to such a wonderful apartment. Why not? I could afford it. But now it was time to go. I gave away all my belongings. I would not need them anymore.

I joined YWAM and officially become a YWAMer (pronounced Y-WAM-ER). It stands for "Youth With A Mission," which is because you're a youth when you join them. But it's okay to stay on even after you're no longer a youth. They don't mind. That's what happened to me. That was over 30 years ago.

9

LOS ANGELES

It was in Los Angeles that I learnt my first lesson on *living by faith*.

Many YWAMers were there as a huge team for the 1984 Olympic Outreach. There were thousands of us from all over the world. I had just finished the first part of my DTS (Discipleship Training School), a six-month programme. We had spent the first three months learning about God, who He is, His character, how to hear His voice and many other subjects. Then we went on outreach to Los Angeles for the second half of the school. This is the part where we are meant to share our faith with other people. It's called evangelism (sharing the Gospel).

Three of us had decided to stay on after the outreach and take a two-week vacation to visit California before flying back to Austria. We were really looking forward to that. But, as the time drew nearer, I realised with horror that the money from my savings account was gone and the two other ladies were no better off. We had virtually nothing, but we couldn't change the airline tickets. We had to stay.

The day after the outreach, everyone else left. We were alone and discouraged, wondering what would become of us. We could no longer stay in the building where we had been lodged during the outreach. We wandered around town aimlessly and ended up in front of a church. It was a Sunday morning and the church service was about to begin. We sat down in the back seats. The pastor started to preach. We barely listened. We were busy worrying. Suddenly the pastor stopped preaching and, in a loud voice, jolted us out of our thoughts: "You three ladies in the back. Please stand up!" He startled us. We hadn't done anything wrong. The pastor asked us who we were. We told him we were from Europe. So he asked the next obvious question.

"What are you doing in the USA?"

"We're with YWAM and just finished our outreach."

"Oh, YWAM, I think I understand."

He then asked us to come up front. That made us really nervous. What had we done?

But he turned to the congregation and said: "These young people have come all the way from Europe to bless our nation." At that time, we were still young. Then he asked a most unexpected question: "Do you need money?" My friend Monika burst into tears and my jaw must have dropped, at which point the pastor asked the church members to come up front and bless us. People came storming up, placing dollar bills into our hands, and some of the ladies were weeping with us. They gave us so much that it fell from our hands onto the floor. It was an absolutely amazing experience. Then the pastor gave us a big American bear-hug and said something that astonished me: "This is not my doing. The Lord told me to do this." I had never experienced God's miraculous provision before. It was an incredible revelation of God's love for us and it stirred my faith. We had the best holiday ever, because we knew, deep in our hearts, that God cared for us!

That was my first experience of living by faith.

10

OUTREACH IN LA

Los Angeles was also my first experience in hearing God's voice during evangelism.

As part of the wider outreach team, our group had been sent to a park in a Hispanic area where we performed. We wore black costumes, our faces were painted white, our lips bright red and our eye-brows as black as can be. It was very hot. The sun had transformed the stage into a frying pan. We wore ballet type slippers and so our feet were scorched. But we bit our lips and kept on. The drama lasted half an hour. So we suffered for Christ for thirty minutes. But we got the people's attention.

At the end, our leaders told us to go and speak to the watching crowds. I was petrified. I had never done this before, so I didn't move. Then my attention was drawn to a lady sitting on the grass at quite a distance. Lying next to her was a baby. I felt this prompting in my spirit: "Go and speak to her." I began to conjure up various excuses like: "She's probably not interested. She's so far away, she most likely didn't even hear what was said. Her baby will wake up and disturb us."

But the promptings of the Holy Spirit did not stop. Finally, I decided to obey and reluctantly dragged my feet in her direction. I was very nervous. As I approached, the lady looked up and beamed at me. "I'm so glad one of you came. I was so hoping you would. I didn't want to wake up my sleeping baby and walk up to your team." I said "Oh" and sat down beside her. She had so many questions. I found myself explaining the Gospel message to a spellbound listener. I finally left her with a written prayer on how to give her life to the Lord. (I was too nervous to pray with her myself). She gave me a beautiful smile and held the paper like a precious stone, saying she would do just that.

And all along her baby had slept peacefully, unaware that his mother was making the biggest decision of her life... one that would probably have lasting effects on its own little life too!

Such was my first experience in listening to the Holy Spirit in evangelism.

11

HEALING IN THE WALDSCHLÖSSL

We returned to the "Waldschlössl", which means "little castle in the woods", except that it wasn't a castle. It was an old hotel and the YWAM Austria base in those days. And once again, we were running a seminar which had started the previous evening. So the "Waldschlössl" was full of people.

I hate having breakfast when there are lots of people around. I don't really want to talk and I certainly don't like answering questions which demand more than a yes or a no answer. So I quietly made my way to the coffee table. Visitors were sitting everywhere, sipping their drinks, chatting, laughing. I hoped I could eventually make it back to my bedroom without anybody noticing me.

Then I felt this tap on my shoulder. I looked around at a young lady. She asked me to pray for her. I mumbled a vague: "I'll do it later" and continued to pour my coffee. I hoped she would leave. But she insisted. "I'm hurting. I'm in pain. Please pray for my healing." I had never prayed for a sick person before. I was not an expert in healing. All I really wanted right now was my coffee. But she kept on insisting, almost in tears. "Please, I've got such a bad stomach ache." So I laid my hands on her and prayed a very short prayer of healing. Then I wandered off to my room, feeling guilty. Poor girl, I thought, she had asked the wrong person.

Later on, I saw her again. I walked up to her, planning to apologise for my lack of empathy and lack of faith.

"How are you doing?"

She gave me a beaming smile.

"Wonderful! My pain left as soon as you prayed. Thank you so much!"

I was speechless. I had no faith for her healing and yet God had healed her, in spite of me.

This is where I learnt that God heals those who believe that He can heal. God doesn't heal because of a mighty prayer. He heals because He loves the sick and cares for them.

And, no, I never apologised.

12

SNAKES

Well, life in the "little castle in the woods" went on. We continued having plenty of guests and so we did a lot of dish-washing. We didn't have a dishwasher.

We also had many guest speakers. One of them told us stories about an orphanage in Eritrea, Africa. The needs seemed tremendous. It wasn't long before I felt that I should go and serve there. Soon others joined in and we planned our outreach trip.

Our first stop would be in Nairobi, Kenya, at a YWAM base. I slept with two other ladies in a tent in the garden. I loved getting up very early in the morning, before sunset. I would creep out and sit under a big tree, watching the sun rise and enjoying wonderful times of fellowship with the Lord. It was my special quiet time spot, and every morning I would see two small black snakes slither along the grass at a distance. I don't particularly care for snakes, but they were small and they seemed inoffensive, so it never bothered me and I would keep on praying and worshipping. Then, one day as we were walking, my friend Klaudia started screaming. As we looked we saw her kicking a black snake which had attached itself to her foot. Immediately the Kenyan workers nearby started yelling:

"Mamba, Mamba!" and set out to kill the snake. I found out that mambas are one of the most venomous snakes in Africa.

I also found out that being ignorant can be such a blessing. I would never have enjoyed such wonderful times under the tree had I known who my slithering neighbours were!

13

ERITREA, AFRICA

It would happen every morning around 5:00 a.m. It was almost as if a hand tapped my shoulder. It would wake me up. There was a sense of holiness in the room. At the other end of our common bedroom, I heard Gabriele move. She too had been awakened. The Lord was calling us.

We both quietly slipped out of the bedroom and one of us would go into the kitchen, while the other would sit outside on the balcony. It was still dark. We lit candles and would start our personal times with God... privileged times of fellowship. Time would fly. The others were still sleeping.

We were in Eritrea, in the late 1980s. The Eritreans were fighting for their independence from Ethiopia. We were visiting an orphanage, ministering to the children during the daytime. At night, despite the curfew, we would creep out and quietly make our way to the place where we ran an underground discipleship course for the local believers.

There was a water shortage in the area. We had only one liter per person for our personal daily wash. In order to save some, we unscrewed the pipe under the sink. The dirty water used for washing would flow into a pail under the sink. This was used for flushing the toilet.

Food too was rare. The United Nations helped provide scarce rations. We only had one type of meat, canned, the famous or infamous corned beef. But it's amazing how one's creative skills develop in times of need. We made the most amazing meals, with incredible variety. Oh, and then there was the cheese which the UN also provided. Granted, it was only and always the same brand, but the Eritreans didn't like cheese. So we got a lot.

I was teaching the young orphans English. Four or five of them would squeeze together on seats meant for only two. They only had one pencil per desk. So I had to wait for each one to write his words down and then pass on the pencil to the next one.

I enjoyed every minute of my time there, so I guess I'm a pioneer.

And it was there that the Lord spoke to me about my future. Early one morning I was praying on the balcony, totally oblivious of the soldier on the other side of the road. He was on duty, his balcony facing mine. Sometimes his gun would point straight at me. It was still curfew time and no-one was allowed on the streets. He probably wondered what I was doing, sitting in the dark with a candle and an open book.

Suddenly I saw a mental picture of Muslim women, veiled women. They were weeping. I instantly knew that the Lord was calling me to reach out to them. I knew nothing about Islam, but that vision changed the course of my life for the next twenty plus years.

14

NOW WHAT?

We returned to the "little castle in the woods," the Wald-schössl. I wondered where I needed to go in order to obey God's call to reach out to Muslim women. There were only a few options in those days. I somehow knew it had to do with North Africa. YWAM had a team working in Morocco at that time, but nowhere else in that region. So could it be Morocco?

I decided to fast and seek God's direction. I fasted seven days. I waited and waited. On the seventh day, God spoke: "Go to Berlin, join this church and ask to speak to the pastor." I was devastated. This had nothing to do with North Africa! I did not want to live in Berlin. I didn't even know this church and even less the pastor. What was going on?

But I knew that I had to obey God. So it was with a heavy heart that I left the little castle in the woods and made my way to Berlin where my mother was now living.

She was happy to see me and welcomed me into her apartment. Little did she know how sad I was. I went to the church, one which was very well known. I asked to meet the main pastor and was given an appointment.

The day of our rendezvous came. I wondered what to say. As I entered the room, Pastor Peter greeted me with a big smile and asked what he could do for me.

"I don't know. The Lord just told me to come and see you."

He stared at me, so I proceeded to explain who I was and that I had been fasting about my future.

Pastor Peter got up and started walking about the office. He did not know either why I was in his office or his church. Finally, he very wisely said: "Let's wait and see. You are welcome to come to our church in the meantime until the Lord clarifies things."

Not only that, but he also offered to let me work for him as a translator.

The thought of staying in Berlin, however, was unbearable to me. So I decided to fast again. Maybe it was just a question of time. Maybe I was meant to go to Morocco after all. I decided to fast for three days. I got up at 6 o'clock, determined to get an answer. At 6:20 the Lord had already replied. No, you are not called to Morocco. That was it. Nothing else. I knew it was pointless to continue asking. It was the shortest fast of my life.

15

GO TO MARSEILLE!

Then, one day, the Lord spoke again. And I wasn't even praying about my future. As far as I knew, my call to missions had been fully burnt on the altar.

But on that day, I heard these words: "Go to Marseille." I did not know this city. In fact, I knew nothing about Marseille, except that it was somewhere in France. Yet somehow I knew instinctively that it was the next step. To my delight, Pastor Peter confirmed that I should go and spy out the land. So I did.

I contacted the YWAM team in Paris. Yes, I could join them. They were just planning an outreach in Marseille!

As the train approached the city of Marseille, my heart started racing. I didn't know why. As I headed out of the railway station, I stopped in my tracks and stared. The sight was magnificent, the huge cathedral on the hill, the majestic stairway leading down to the streets.

As I walked down I noticed something else. There were North Africans everywhere. Muslim men, women and children. I found out that Marseille had the largest percentage of North African Muslims in France, maybe even in Europe. Suddenly I understood why God had not called me to North Africa. I was meant to come here.

And I fell in love with Marseille. I knew that this was where God was calling me.

To my surprise and joy, Pastor Peter and the entire eldership decided to send me out as a missionary from their church. I was anointed and appointed to go! This church supported and prayed for me for over twenty years.

I had spent less than a year in Berlin.

16

PARIS

I first moved to Paris prior to living in Marseille. That was in 1989. I joined the YWAM team there and worked in our Schools of Evangelism as well as the Paris outreach team for a few years.

One day I attended a church in Paris. I had never been there before. The service was in full swing. I was enjoying the worship. I absent-mindedly looked around the crowd and noticed this man on the other side of the room. He seemed sad, looking at the floor.

Then God spoke.

"Tell him to give his life to Me now. Today is the day."

I stared at him. I did not know him. Who was he? Maybe he was a dedicated Christian? Maybe he was an elder? Or worse still, maybe he was the pastor? I did not want to budge. I was afraid of making a fool of myself.

But the Holy Spirit kept on nudging me. Reluctantly I made my way up to the man. I mumbled a vague:

"I believe God has a word for you. He says you need to do it today. I mean, make the decision." I did not dare tell him to give his life to God.

I was sweating as I walked back to my seat. What had I

done? The man just kept staring at the floor.

The worship time ended. Almost immediately the man jumped up and ran to the front. He grabbed the microphone. "Oh no, it was the pastor. How embarrassing." I dared not look.

Then the man spoke. He had recently been approached by Christians who had shared the Gospel with him. They had invited him to church. He had not slept the night before, wondering whether Jesus would really accept him too. He had been crying out to God. "If you are willing to accept me, then please tell me personally!"

He then continued, "This morning, God spoke to me personally through someone in this room. I am to give my life to Him today. So I want to be baptised *now!*"

I was amazed at the reaction of the pastor of the church. The whole church service was changed. The baptismal pool was prepared and the man was baptised right then and there.

And I was so relieved.

17

THE INDIAN AND THE BACKSLIDER

A man suddenly appeared at the doorway, blocking the sunlight. He stood there, motionless, unsure of whether to enter or not. We were in our coffee shop in Belleville, Paris.

I walked up and asked if I could help him. He seemed confused and pulled out a piece of paper. I recognised our flyer, the one inviting people to visit our Christian coffee shop

"Someone gave me this a few days ago. I stuck the paper in my pocket and forgot about it. But this morning I pulled it out and suddenly there was this strong urge to come here. I can't explain it, but I feel that you have a story to tell me." He was frowning. He was trying to figure it out. He was clearly not European. Maybe Indian or Pakistani? I did not know either what story he was referring too, so I asked him the next best question.

"Well, have you heard about Jesus?"

"Jesus? No."

"The cross? Have you heard about Jesus and the cross?"

"No, never. What cross?"

I was amazed. We were in Europe and yet this man had never even heard the name of Jesus.

"Well, I think I do have a story to tell you. Follow me." We sat down and I told him the story, from Genesis to the Cross and the Resurrection. He was staring at me, taking in every word. At the end, he murmured wistfully: "This is the most beautiful story I have ever heard!"

I asked if he wanted to pray, but it was too soon, of course. How silly of me. It takes time to understand.

"Not yet. I am from India. Only an hour ago I had never even heard of Jesus. I need to first digest this incredible story." And then he left, the Indian who had been led into our coffee shop by the Holy Spirit.

This reminded me then of the Frenchman we had met. We were doing street evangelism on a little side street off Place Beaubourg in Paris. Jean-Claude, my colleague, and I were chatting when this man appeared. "I need to tell you something. I was at home when I suddenly I felt this strange urge to go out. I somehow ended up at the Place Beaubourg where I wandered around until I felt to turn into this street. There I heard your singing and preaching and was drawn to it. As I stood and listened, I knew instantly why I was here. I am a backslider. I have known Jesus. I know that it is the Holy Spirit who has led me to you. I want to rededicate my life to Jesus. Will you please pray with me?" Of course!

What a privilege to be around when the Holy Spirit sends you seekers!

18

HEARING GOD'S VOICE

We prayed as we walked along Marseille's main street, the famous "Canebière." There was nothing else we could do at this point.

We were looking for lodging for about 25 young people for our planned summer evangelistic event. We did not have the right contacts and in a couple of days, we would have to return to Paris.

We asked the Lord to speak to us, to guide us to the right person. A man's name came to my mind. My fellow YWAMer thought of a church, a French Reformed Church (ERF).

We fumbled through a booklet which listed about 50 churches in Marseille. To our amazement, the name I had received was that of a pastor from a French Reformed Church! Now we were excited. We checked the address and realised it was at walking distance from where we were.

Within less than 15 minutes we were ringing the doorbell of this church. The door was opened by the pastor himself. It was a Wednesday afternoon. The pastor informed us that he was only available for appointments on Wednesday afternoons. We were lucky, he said.

We shared our need. "Yes, yes." He understood. Wonderful

that young people were planning to come and evangelise this needy city. He knew where we could lodge them. The ERF also had a preschool. It would be closed in the summer and the classrooms would be available. He gave us the name of the person who was in charge. "You will most likely not get to see him now. He is a very busy doctor. However, if and when you do see him, do tell him I am sending you with the request that he help you."

We were so grateful for this pastor's welcome and readiness to help us. We decided to try and call the doctor and leave a message. Maybe, just maybe, he would be available to see us before we had to leave the city. We dialed his number. Almost immediately someone answered. He was home. He did not live far from where we were calling and he was available.

A few minutes later we sat at a coffee shop and talked. Of course he would help us. He could show us the school building right away. Did we have time?

That school building blessed us for many a summer season for our evangelistic campaigns.

God had miraculously provided! He had spoken and directed. We were blessed.

I still lived in Paris at that time. It was 1990.

19

JERRY

After living in Paris for almost three years, I moved down to the YWAM base in the south of France, in a little town called Saint Paul-Trois-Chateaux, which either means, Saint Paul had three castles, or Saint Paul and the three castles. Except that there are no castles there and the apostle Paul never owned a castle. Believe me!

I shared an apartment with a fellow YWAMer. One evening we heard this desperate mewing. Looking down from our third floor apartment, we saw a cat. We went down and took a closer look. She looked absolutely famished. So we brought her home and fed her. Deeply content, she decided to stay.

Then we heard another mewing. This time it was the voice of a very young kitten. We stared at the cat we had just picked up, wondering if she was the mama. But she did not move, showed no signs of interest whatsoever. So we figured the kitten's mother was probably not far away.

But the little kitten mewed all evening, all night and all morning. It finally dawned on me that he was truly abandoned, so I went down and started looking for him. I blindly groped around in the bush surrounding our community garden and then picked up this little furry creature. It was barely a week old, eyes still glued together, unable to walk, unable to fend for itself.

As I carried this crying kitten up the stairs, I wondered how the adult cat who had just moved into our home would react. She saw the kitten, picked him up and immediately started caring for him. She was the mama. Had she planned it all? And so little Jerry moved into his new home.

It reminded me of the importance of persevering prayer. Sometimes the waiting seems too long, unbearably long. We believe God does not hear us or even care about us. But He does, and just when we think we cannot hang in there any longer, He comes and picks us up.

And that was the beginning of a 19-year *partnership* between me and Jerry. I did the shopping, cleaning, feeding, while Jerry did the sleeping, eating, purring.

Jerry eventually moved with me to Marseille.

20

I WILL KILL YOU!

"I will find you and I will kill you!"

Khadija's brother was screaming into the phone at his sister. We both looked at each other. Khadija had committed the unacceptable. She had left her former faith in order to embrace Christianity. Her family had already ostracised her, but her older brother felt duty-bound to restore the family's honour. She had to renounce her new-found beliefs and return to her previous faith or he would kill her. Fortunately, he was in prison. She was safe, for now. (Khadija eventually married a wonderful Christian man, also formerly from the same religious background. From then on, her family left her alone. She was no longer their responsibility.)

We shared an apartment in a North African residential section of town. We met many neighbours and they were delighted to see us play, sing and care for their little ones. Most of these mothers were what we call: the *first generation,* meaning that they were born and raised in North Africa before moving to France as adults. So their lifestyle was no different than what they had been used to in their home countries. Their only entertainment was going to the marketplace or visiting each other's homes. Going out to a coffee shop, for a meal to a restaurant, or the cinema without a male escort from the family was out of the question. It was culturally inappropriate. So we met with them in their homes. In that context, I learnt about Folk Islam or non-traditional Islam.

I had already learnt from Khadija about how many women from North Africa are involved in the occult and suffer from demonic manifestations. Then one day, I got even more first-hand experience.

I knocked at the door of my friend, a lovely Tunisian lady. Her little boy answered.

"Mama's in the bedroom." I followed him in and found his mother kneeling on the floor. She was hammering away. The bed was pushed aside.

"What's up, my friend?"

"I have just killed a chicken and am burying his head inside the cement right here where my husband sleeps. I am doing it so that he will stop beating me."

My heart broke for her. These women have little hope that their prayers for help, for protection or comfort will be answered. It is common knowledge that their deity prefers men and, according to some of their thoughts, beating a wife is not wrong. So the women resort to sorcery, hoping that it will bring them relief from their problems.

I pulled her aside and asked if I could pray for her. She nodded and as I laid my hands on her shoulders, God ministered to her broken soul. She wept bitterly. Muslim women, like all of us, desperately need a touch of God's love and they are very receptive to prayer.

21

FINALLY . . . .

I finally moved to Marseille in 1996. I ended up in a not so nice area of town where prostitution and drugs were rampant. Apart from that, it was a quaint little neighbourhood. Actually, it was the oldest section of Marseille, packed with history. It was here that Marseille had been founded over 2700 years ago.

I lived near and worked with a church that believed in helping the down and out. There were many of them and we had to be on our toes. Church services were always full of unexpected surprises.

There was Bruce of course, the German shepherd belonging to a prostitute. He was a rough dog. His job as a bodyguard for his mistress was a tough one. He would flop down in the aisle during church services. People carefully crept around him or cautiously stepped over him. No-one dared tread on him.

I had found a small apartment close to the church, but it was dark and I wanted something sunnier. I knew that I needed another miracle, as landlords in France do not want tenants who do not receive pay checks. The explanation of regular donations given to missionaries does not impress them. I had been turned down at every housing agency I entered until I had found this one. By now my heart was aching for a sunny place with more light.

One day I had lunch with a pastor and his wife. I mentioned my desire, not expecting anything more than a nod and a promise to pray for me. To my surprise, they told me that an apartment was available right above theirs. The apartment belonged to the pastor's uncle. Did I want to see it? We lost no time and marched up to the 5th floor. As I entered, I gasped. I had seen this apartment a few years ago. Someone had shown it to me and I had immediately fallen in love with it. Such a pretty place, and to top it all, a beautiful sunny terrace.

On that day I had heard the Lord say: "One day you will live here." For some strange reason I had totally forgotten this, but the Lord had not!

The owners were a retired pastor and his wife. They were delighted to rent it out to a missionary and I got the keys! God had kept His promise!

Around that same time more YWAMers had started coming. Soon we were a dozen people.

For 10 years our team worked in the city. We ran seminars and training programmes in various churches. Some ministered in the more difficult areas of Marseille where the economic and housing needs were rampant. Others were involved in intercession, discipleship or church planting. We hosted many short term teams and did a lot of street evangelism. Those of us who were called to the North African nations crossed the Mediterranean on numerous occasions.

And my sunny apartment became the YWAM Marseille administrative headquarters as well as hosting our team meetings.

22

IF YOU ONLY KNEW!

He was standing there in the distance, almost in the dark. We had just finished an outreach on the beach in Marseille. The sun was setting and it was time to pack up and go.

I had noticed the man. He had obviously heard everything, the testimonies, the preaching. I felt I should talk to him. So I slowly wandered up to him across the beach, enjoying the feel of sand under my bare feet.

I never lose time with small talk when I know that people have listened during an evangelistic outreach.

"Would you like to talk about God?"

"Absolutely not. Not interested." There was no smile. Almost a scowl.

I shrugged my shoulders and turned around. No point in insisting. I don't believe in Bible bashing.

"No, please. Do come back."

I turned back, surprised. He looked nervous. He apologised for his rudeness. "Please talk to me," he said. "Tell me about Jesus."

So I did. I could sense that he was receptive. There was something like a holy silence around us as I shared the Gospel message. And then he told me.

"If you only knew!" He had been extremely discouraged. He did not think he could go on with his life and had decided to walk up to the beach. It was to be his final walk, one final look at the world.

But then he saw us and something made him stop and watch.

He looked at me and smiled.

"I want to thank you for talking to me. I will go back home. I now have a reason to live."

I watched him walk away and wondered. What if I had not wandered over to speak to that lonely stranger? It was a sobering thought.

23

THAT TRIBE

I was in a very poor village high up in the mountains of a Muslim nation in Africa visiting a small group of Christians. These people had so little, but so much love for Jesus. When I asked if I could bring them something back from France on my next trip, there was silence for a while. Then, timidly, one person spoke up.

"Could you bring us a New Testament? In our language?"

Only the New Testament had been translated into their mother tongue at that time and it was printed in France. So we did. We wrapped them up individually to look like presents in order to facilitate border crossings. We only brought a few each time. These New Testaments were received and cherished like gold.

I remembered my first trip to this nation. I was walking along the dusty streets of a small town, admiring the local pottery when I first saw it, the poster of the Campus Crusade Jesus film, showing the portrait of the actor playing the role of Jesus. This was an unheard of thing in a Muslim nation. Then I saw more of them, proudly displayed on the doors of various little shops. I asked the lady who accompanied me: "Are your people not afraid of openly showing this poster?"

"We do not care. It is a film in our language. Our language !"

I suddenly realised the importance of language. Despite centuries of Arabic-Islamic domination, this particular tribe had held fiercely to their language, transmitting it orally from generation to generation.

After that, I often heard the following testimony: As Muslims, these people would perform their ritualistic prayers in Arabic, as dictated by Islam. But they deeply resented it. Why could they not pray in their own language?

When they heard that Jesus loves their mother-tongue, the shackles of ethnic rule fell.

A deep sense of dignity arose. They were loved, with their language, their culture, their dances, their music, their dress code. They were loved for who they were.

Never underestimate the power of language.

24

THE LITTLE VILLAGE IN THE MOUNTAINS

It was my second trip into this region, across the Mediterranean. The pastors came to pick us up at the airport. We thankfully made it through customs. Each one of us had carried a few Bibles wrapped up as gifts in our suitcases. But as we approached the pastors, soldiers came rushing up. They seemed nervous.

I hoped they were not here to stop us, but after a while they let us go. The situation in the country was not safe. There were terrorists about and the soldiers had asked the pastors to be extra careful. They did not want diplomatic tensions with other nations. There were three of us, from three different western countries.

We left the airport and drove up a mountainous road. It was a trip that took several hours. Suddenly, one of the pastors turned around and shouted : "Pray! Now!" So we did, though we wondered why.

They explained later on. At specific spots there were often roadblocks, some were military, some were fake. Terrorists, dressed as soldiers, would block the road, forcing the people to get out of their cars, only to kill them. More often than not, they would cut their throats. Then they would send the cars crashing down the deep valley. For some strange reason this caused me no fear. I was filled with an unusual sense of peace, a knowing that it was going to be alright. God's grace was there, carrying us.

We arrived in a little mountain village. It was our first visit there. The pastor and elders invited us to sit down. They were friendly, but I could sense a certain annoyance.

"So, are you also here to invite us to join your church movement or organisation as some others have? And are you also planning to pay for our training ?"

How funny. I laughed.

"Of course not. YWAM doesn't pay for people to join our training programmes or our mission. The students have to pay their own school fees. And you can only join us if you have a call for missions and if you are willing to live by faith."

"What do you mean, living by faith?"

"It means that we do not get salaries. We must trust God to provide for our needs. We pray for finances to arrive. We need to learn to be content whether living in plenty or in want."

Their confused faces broke out into big smiles.

"Wow! We like that! That is good."

They adopted us. It was the beginning of a beautiful friendship.

25

THE VALUE OF WOMEN

The pastor pulled me aside. I wondered what he would ask me. I had prepared for this trip. I had prayed and prayed. I did not know if I would be asked to preach, but I had asked the Lord if He had a message for the women. And the Lord laid on my heart the message of the value of women. He gave me no other message.

So I had studied, I had pored over the Scriptures on Jesus and his interactions with women. I studied the cultural background of that time. The more I read, the more I rejoiced. It fit in perfectly with the cultural background of Muslim peoples.

My heart ached for these women. They were poor, uneducated, but had such servant hearts. So hard-working, fetching water from the fountain, plucking feathers off a chicken before cooking it. They had so little, but they shared so generously. And they loved Jesus.

I heard the pastor speak. "I want you to teach the women. We are having problems with them."

I groaned inwardly. I was in a Muslim nation, in a Muslim village, speaking to a former Muslim man. What was he going to say?

I held my breath as he explained.

"We, the men, go around visiting homes in the village, sharing the Gospel message. Men are coming to the Lord, but not the women. And our wives, those who know Jesus, are afraid to come with us. They do not believe that they are able to minister. They are afraid to share the Gospel, afraid to pray for other women. Please, tell our women that they have great value in God's eyes and that He wants to use them."

I could not believe what I heard. I was coming from France, where many churches still believe that women should not be involved in ministry! And here, high up in the mountains, in a little Muslim village, the Holy Spirit was moving. He was calling poor, uneducated women to serve Him. What an honour to be chosen to encourage them. And how thankful I was that I had been prompted to prepare that very message.

So I shared what the Lord had taught me and then I prayed for each of the women. Towards the end, the pastor quietly opened the door which housed our meeting. He popped in his head, only to disappear as quickly as he had come. It happened several times and I wondered what was going on.

I soon found out. It was late and the men were hungry. The pastor had come to ask the women to hurry up and prepare the meal, but each time, he had felt the strong presence of the Holy Spirit. He did not dare interrupt. Finally, the men decided to prepare the meal themselves. And not only that, they decided to bless the women and serve them. It was an unheard of thing in that culture. The women giggled and were nervous. They were asked to sit down and be served, but they could not. They jumped up and started serving. We all ended up laughing.

26

THE FLOWER GIRL

We were high up in the mountains again. I was teaching the women and I was so thankful for the Holy Spirit. He was filling my mouth. What an honour to be used by Him!

The ladies were so attentive, so thirsty for more of God. They challenged me. They did not want a pause during the teachings. I did. They did not mind the cold. I sure did. But who was I to complain? I was only here for a week. This was their ongoing life. So I continued. I noticed one lady in particular. She was shivering. No wonder, I thought, it was so cold. No, they did not have heating in these little mountainous villages in this nation across the Mediterranean. It was a luxury they could not afford.

At the end of my teaching the ladies lined up. They wanted prayer, each one individually. I prayed silently in desperation. I wanted each one to be blessed. I knew that without the Holy Spirit I would have nothing to give. But the Lord blessed and gave me prophetic words for each woman. There were words of encouragement, but also words to go forth and serve Him, each one according to their gifts.

The last person was the shivering lady. I felt so sorry for her. Then, to my horror, a very tender word came to my mind.

Surely the Lord had something better to say to her. But nothing else came. Sadly, I told her what the Holy Spirit had impressed upon my mind.

"The Lord says that He is not asking you to do anything for Him. He just loves you for who you are. You are like a beautiful flower for Him. You are His beautiful flower!"

I had nothing more to say. The lady burst into tears. It saddened me even more.

But then the translator spoke. The lady came from another village. She had come specifically for the meeting. She was a young Christian. She lived in a majority Muslim village (like every other village in that nation). She did not have the courage to share her faith with others. Not yet. Would God ask her to do something like that? She just wanted to be with God. That was why she was shivering.

Her tears were not tears of sadness, but of deep relief. I was so relieved too. I asked for her name.

"Ourida"

"What does it mean?"

"It means flower!"

It made me smile. Such a revelation of God's tender care for his precious, fearful *flower*. His purpose, above all things, is to be our Father, not our employer.

27

BORN AGAIN

We wondered what was going on. The pastor and elders were praying fervently with the young woman, taking authority over an evil spirit. It lasted a long time. Eventually, they gave up and the church service resumed. The young lady slowly made her way down to the back of the church. Her head was downcast. She was shaking.

We were in the mountains again, in a Muslim nation. My co-labourer, Robert, suggested I go and pray for her. I was hurting for her but did not know what I could better than the leaders of her church. By now the girl had quietly slipped out of the church building. I followed her. She was leaning against a wall. Her face was so fearful, so desperate. I invited her to follow me into an adjoining room, accompanied by a translator.

She did indeed seem to be held prisoner by an evil spirit. She could not look at me, her eyes flicked back and forth. I was filled with compassion for her. Suddenly I felt led to ask her about her conversion experience.

"There were evil spirits in the house and I was so afraid. Someone told me that I needed to ask Jesus to help me."

"That is true. Jesus can help you. But what else do you know about Jesus?"

"Nothing else."

She did not know. She had prayed to accept Jesus without fully understanding. So I shared the Gospel message with her: the Cross, Jesus, repentance. I asked her if she wanted to receive Jesus and if she was willing to repent. She was.

She bowed her head and we prayed.

Then she lifted her head and looked at me. I could hardly believe what I was seeing. Her eyes were beaming. The fear was gone. The light was there. The darkness was no more. She was truly born again, freed from bondage.

The pastor walked in. He was amazed.

"What did you do?"

"Nothing. She met Jesus and He set her free."

28

JUBILEE GIFT

In a few months I was going to turn fifty. As I prayed one February morning, I felt directed to a Scripture in Leviticus 25 on the year of Jubilee, the 50th anniversary. The Jubilee was also the year for one's sold property to be returned to him. I did not have property anywhere, but I knew instantly that the Lord was telling me to return to Mauritius. I was to enjoy my year of Jubilee by returning *home*. But how? I had not returned since my conversion 25 years ago. And I had since put Mauritius and my former life and friends on the back burner.

At the same time, I was also going through one of the most difficult times in my life. A division had come into our team, triggered off by slander against me. It lasted years. I was devastated by this. So when the Lord told me that he wanted to bless me for my "jubilee," it was like balm on a gaping wound.

The months went by. Somehow I forgot about the trip to Mauritius. I even wondered if I had heard the Lord correctly. Then, shortly before my birthday in September, I received a phone call. It was so unexpected that I almost fell off my chair. My dear childhood friend, Patricia, was on the line.

"When are you coming to visit us?"

What a delight to hear her voice! I had not spoken to her for so many years. Then I remembered what the Lord had told me and heard myself saying the impossible.

"I'm coming. I'll be there before the end of the year."

I put the phone down. I had no money for such a trip, but I knew I would go.

Only a couple of weeks later, I received another phone call. A team member asked me if I would be interested in going out for a meal with a traveling businessman who wanted to get to know a few missionaries. *Why not,* I thought. No harm in going out for a meal.

The next day we had lunch in a lovely restaurant. The man wanted to know as much as possible about myself and my ministry. Towards the end of the meal, he spoke.

"I believe that I am meant to buy you an airline ticket."

I stared at him. At first, I was speechless.

Finally I asked: "What kind of a ticket? I mean, a flight within Europe?"

"No, a flight to anywhere in the world. All the way to New Zealand if you wish."

So I dared to tell him about Mauritius and my desire to go there.

"OK. Let's do it." He got up and dragged me to the nearest travel agency. He wanted to book the flight right then and there. And he did. In November I was on my plane to Mauritius.

29

MIRACULOUS HEALING

I rushed into the kitchen as I heard him vomit. I could not believe what I was seeing. Jerry, my cat, was violently sick, throwing up blood, amongst other things.

Within minutes I was on my way to the vet. After checking him, the vet strongly suggested putting Jerry to sleep. A scanner had shown that he had a multitude of cancerous tumours, including one which totally blocked his urinary and bowel tracts. He was in terrible pain. Nothing could be done. The vet was adamant. It was best to put him out of his agony.

Jerry was about 12 years old, not quite the age to die yet for a cat. For some strange reason, I chose to take him back home, much to the vet's disgust. I carefully placed him on my bed and ran down to fetch my neighbour, Eugene, a man of prayer. I asked him to pray for Jerry. We both laid hands on my cat and prayed for his healing.

I then had to attend to arriving guests, as it had been too late to postpone their coming. We settled into the kitchen for our planned meeting. I hated leaving my dying cat alone in the bedroom. He was breathing heavily, unable to move, still obviously in great pain. I tried to focus on our meeting, trying to contain my anxiety, despite our prayers.

Then I heard a familiar sound, scratching in the litter-box. Jerry was up. He had gotten off the bed and made his way out onto the terrace. Both his urinary tract and bowels were functioning. I saw a strange green substance in the litter-box. I did not inspect it any further. I instantly knew that whatever had blocked Jerry's urinary and bowel tracts had just been miraculously evacuated.

By evening Jerry was fine. He had been healed and he lived many more happy years!

30

THE GIFT OF LIFE

She was beaming. She had the happiest face, and I wondered what made her so joyful.

But I need to backtrack. It all started during one of our first trips to this Muslim nation. We were up in the mountains, in a small village, visiting a group of believers. A young couple came to us asking for prayer. They had tried to have children, but each of their three babies had been stillborn after seven months of pregnancy. Three deaths, always at the same age. It was obvious that it was a curse. We prayed for them, took authority over evil and broke the curse, by faith. Then we left.

Two years later, I was visiting again. I was holding a ladies' meeting. As I was teaching, I noticed one young woman in particular, the smiling one, the happy one.

After the meeting, she walked up to me.

"Do you remember me?"

I was afraid that I did not. So she reminded me.

"You and your co-labourers prayed for me."

Then she held up a pretty little girl in front of her. "Here she is, the miracle girl. God has provided!"

She then proceeded to tell me the rest of the story. The little baby was born. All had gone so well. She and her husband were delighted. God had answered our prayers. The curse had indeed been broken, just as we had prayed.

But it had not been without another battle. While she was still in the hospital with her little baby sleeping peacefully beside her, she had sensed an evil presence.

It was in the corridor, coming closer. But she had learnt how to fight evil. She took authority and the lurking creature wandered off. Her baby was safe. The spirit of death had no power against the name of Jesus.

I smiled at the happy mother and the cute little girl. God is still the God of mighty miracles!

31

SHOULD I OR SHOULD I NOT?

Rebecca was concerned. She wanted to do God's will. A man had proposed to her. Was he the right husband for her? She asked me to pray with her.

We were up in the mountains. We huddled closer in the building that served as the church. It was cold, as usual. I had known Rebecca for several years. She loved the Lord with all her heart.

Clasping hands, we prayed: "Lord, you know best. We ask that you give Rebecca peace. We ask for signs from you. Is this man the right one for her?"

Suddenly the whole earth shook. The building trembled. So did we. We ran out, just like everybody else. In the distance we saw smoke in the mountains. It was an earthquake. It had shaken the ground. Finally everything quieted down. We waited a bit and then wandered back into the church.

We held hands, one more time. "Should I or should I not marry this man, Lord?" Rebecca prayed.

Again the earth shook. And once again we ran out. Yes, it was another quake! We later found out that it had affected the entire northern part of that nation. The coastal regions were badly damaged, buildings had collapsed. But here, high up in the mountains we were safe, except for the tremors.

Rebecca was as white as a sheet. She looked at me. "I think God does not want me to marry this man. I don't need another sign."

A few years later, she met another man, her future husband. And they lived happily ever after....

Please note: I am not saying that God *purposely* ordained an earthquake causing much damage just in order to answer Rebecca's prayer. But, He had definitely used it as a sign for Rebecca.

32

LET'S DO IT!

"I want that man to come to my nation." Mahmoud's loud voice boomed across the spacious dining hall. We were in a hotel, on an island. I was attending a conference for workers in Muslim nations. And no, I won't tell you where we met. I have never attended conferences which required such high security measures. Three passwords were needed before you could even register and I am pretty sure that no James Bond could ever find us.

Mahmoud strode towards me, his voice crying out for all to hear. I wondered who he was talking about. Then it dawned on me. Several months prior, I had given him a copy of Loren Cunningham's book "Is that really you, Lord?" This book describes the founding of YWAM but also includes a very practical, encouraging teaching on hearing God's voice and obeying Him.

Was Mahmoud angry or something?

"Why do you want Loren C. to come?"

"I want him to teach us all he has learnt about hearing God's voice."

I hesitated: "I doubt that he will obtain a visa, more likely a fatwa."

One cannot enter this nation without a visa and it's not easy to obtain. Hosts are put under surveillance and names of invitees are carefully screened and Google searched. And I was pretty sure that Loren's name pops up about 100 times, causing an avalanche of fatwas against him.

A fatwa is a decree made by elders of Islam. If one has been pronounced against someone, it means that he has been put on the *wanted* list to be killed because of a serious offense. Like, for instance, sending thousands of people all over the world to preach the Gospel and causing people to turn away from their former faith in order to embrace Christianity. For them that is a very serious offense demanding a fatwa.

Mahmoud was disappointed. Of course not. He didn't want Loren to be beheaded in his country.

"Do you specifically want to speak to Loren? Or is it the teaching on hearing God's voice? If it is his teachings you want, then we have another solution." I explained about our YWAM Discipleship Training School (DTS).

"You know, all of us in YWAM go through training to hear God's voice in intercession, evangelism, and in seeking His will for our lives. We can run such a training programme."

His face broke out into a smile. "You can? Really? Then, let's do it. Let's run that school!"

And that was the beginning of a mighty adventure.

33

MINI-DTS

A regular six-month school was out of the question for security reasons. But a short one, a few weeks, that was feasible. And so we planned our first ever YWAM mini-DTS in this nation. We fixed the dates for June 2006.

By the way, other organisations were also involved in that nation, doing wonderful undercover work. And the local pastors were doing a great job leading their rapidly growing churches with the best teacher, the Holy Spirit. We felt honoured to be a small part of what the Lord was doing.

I knew it was meant to be now. There was a sense of urgency. We had heard about the new law. The government was clamping down on churches, proselytism was condemned more so than ever before. Would they grant us the visas?

Everything else, however, started falling into place. Annett and Naceera wanted to collaborate with me. And I needed faithful, spirit-filled, on-fire fellow believers. They were perfect. Annett, the wise one, kind and compassionate, and Naceera, the laughing optimist, with a high dose of faith. Nothing was impossible for her God. Nothing.

By the way, isn't that ironic? Three ladies leading a biblical training programme for men and women in a Muslim nation? I just know that God loves these types of situations.

Of course, we could not communicate using emails, or phones. So Ferhat, a brother who had dual citizenship, became our faithful postman. He was able to travel back and forth without raising any suspicion. He was our communicator, but also our advisor. He knew how to weave in and out of both cultures with great ease. It was good to have him.

We needed a place where we could host the school, a safe house, away from prying eyes. The original plan had been to run the school in one of the villages high up in the mountains. But with the new law, fear had crept in, and also caution. The elders there felt that it was unwise. It could cause major difficulties for the church as a whole. We understood, but we were running out of time.

Then the Lord provided miraculously.

Only a few weeks prior to the start of our school a brother talked to Ferhat. He had a beach house on the Mediterranean. Maybe it could be used for the school? They went to check it out. As soon as they walked into the building, the Spirit of the Lord fell mightily upon them and they started weeping for joy. They left convinced that this was the Lord's chosen safe house.

We had 18 students, hand-picked by the pastors from about 8 churches. They sent us their best. We could not accept more, despite many demands. The house was small, the guys would have to sleep on the roof, counting the stars, literally.

We arrived one week earlier for preparations, such as getting the house cleaned up, shopping, praying.

There was such excitement in the air. Speakers had all agreed to come. We knew the students could hardly wait to embark on this new adventure. They were so hungry for spiritual food. We were filled with high hopes. I felt God's hand upon us. We had received our visas. Funds had miraculously arrived, generous donations which would cover all expenses. We were on our way.

Upon arrival at the airport, we were picked up by a minivan. We stacked our luggage into the vehicle and drove off. Pretty soon it was lunch-time. We parked, and wandered off into a small restaurant. We could see our van from a distance.

Suddenly I felt uncomfortable. This strange inkling that I should return to our vehicle and get my satchel, the one which had all the sensitive information concerning the training programme. I went and picked it up and returned to finish my lunch.

Less than an hour later we returned, and our hearts sunk. The van had been broken in. We had been cleverly robbed of all our belongings. All our suitcases were gone. We had been plundered!

It was a terrible blow. A real kill-joy. All our clothes, gifts, air mattresses, sleeping bags, food and, more importantly, Annett's medication. She was under treatment after chemotherapy. We sat and wept.

Our only consolation was the satchel that I had felt led to recuperate. It would have been a disaster had it fallen into the wrong hands. We would have had to cancel the school immediately for security reasons.

We got into the vehicle with heavy hearts. We knew that it was only the enemy's last desperate attempt to stop us, but it wasn't fun. Our local friends were filled with compassion. Wherever we stopped on the way, their homes and hearts opened to us. They tried to comfort us and gave us the little they had: a box of dates, a bottle of olive oil, a few spare clothes. We were humbled.

After that, our spirits rose again. We prayed. We trusted and things got better. Annett managed to phone her husband and he organised for medication to be sent on with our first speaker. Our joy returned. Never mind the lost items.

We inspected the house and surroundings. How absolutely perfect! There were fields all around us. A few houses too, but they were empty. It was not the holiday season yet. We were alone. Well, almost, in the fields were sheep. They roamed and grazed peacefully. We never saw the shepherds. The sheep were our only visible neighbours. But they would never betray us.

We wandered down to the Mediterranean. It was only a short walk. What a delight! The students would be able to go swimming, or walk and pray on the beach. What a perfect place! I know, I already wrote that. But, honestly, God had provided the best safe house.

The students arrived. They were as excited as we were. We, as staff ladies, shared one bedroom, the girl students had the other room. Some of the men slept in the living/dining/meeting room, which was cleverly transformed into a bedroom every night. The rest of them slept on the roof. Yes, there were more men than women in this class.

I have worked in various discipleship schools, but this was the best one I had ever led. The students were desperate for teaching. There was no need to summon them to the classroom. They were there before me. They were always waiting, asking for more and more. Such a thirst. I loved every minute of it, the teaching, the organising, the leading. The thrill of new speakers arriving safely. Even the hiding, being careful. It was fun because somehow I felt that even God was laughing, smiling.

The school ended. We left rejoicing over all we had experienced together. It had been good, more than good. In fact, it had been awesome!

Sometime later, I went to the consulate in order to get another visa. I wanted to see my students again. The employee at the visa section frowned as he looked at his computer. He then stormed out of the office. After a while, he returned. He was angry. My request was denied. It was over.

I mourned over this for several years. I had grown to love these people. I had learnt so much from them, through them, their lifestyle, their sacrificial giving. I had lost a family.

Years went by. God healed my heart. I can now look back with joy over what happened. I count it a privilege to have witnessed the Lord's work among that people-group and in that nation.

34

THE PROPHETIC ANOINTING

Some friends and I were in California, the Redding area, in 2008. Bethel church was holding an open service right there on the beach for anyone to join in. What a grand idea!

By now everyone had heard of the strong prophetic anointing on that church. So I was delighted when two young Bethel men came up to me after the service. They asked if they could pray for me. Of course. I was going through a difficult season in my life and all prayers and especially prophetic words were more than welcome.

I stretched out my hands, closed my eyes and waited. Nothing happened. I finally opened my eyes and saw the two men staring at me.

"Excuse me," they said, "but who are you?"

"Oh, I'm a missionary."

"A missionary! Wow! Could you please pray for us?"

I was taken aback. What a strange turn of events. But then, why not. I could pray for them and then they could pray for me afterwards.

As I laid hands on the first young man, a powerful prophetic anointing came upon me. It surprised me. Words came gushing out of my mouth. They came forth with power. The young man fell over backwards, slain in the Spirit. He had an obvious call to missions.

The second young man was watching intently. I could sense his expectation. I hoped he would be blessed too. I wasn't sure. But again, prophetic words came blurting out of my mouth. A few seconds later, he too was slain in the Spirit. He also had a clear call to serve God in missions.

I stared at them both, lying there on the sandy beach. They were knocked out. I knew there was no point waiting for them to recuperate. I was not going to receive prayer for myself tonight.

I slowly wandered back towards my friends. "Well, were you blessed? Did you get prophetic words?"

"I guess I did."

35

SUPERNATURAL HEALING
MARSEILLE

The hotel restaurant was packed. We had all been invited to attend a seminar on healing. After the meal, the speaker went up front. He taught on physical healing, on faith, and then asked for a volunteer. Our dear friend Anne-Marie got up. She had experienced a bad car accident which had damaged her backbone. She was in pain from the neck downwards. Sitting was difficult, kneeling was impossible.

We waited with expectancy. What would happen? How was the Lord going to move?

The speaker started praying for her. He prayed for a long time. Nothing happened. I was saddened for Anne-Marie. The speaker eventually asked for another volunteer to come forward. He explained that sometimes God does not heal immediately. Anne-Marie was still sitting on the platform. Suddenly the Lord spoke to me: "Go up and pray for her."

Oh no, she's sitting up front. Surely you don't expect me to just walk up and pray for her?

"Yes, I want you to go and pray for her." So I did. A friend, Josephine, joined me. We both prayed. But nothing happened.

Eventually, we helped Anne-Marie return to the table. As

soon as she sat down, the Lord gave me a picture of a power-ful metallic hand clasping Anne-Marie's neck. That hand was blocking her every move. I asked her if this meant anything to her. She immediately said yes. That was exactly what she felt, a metallic hand causing her great pain. The Lord spoke again:

"It is demonic and needs to be broken off."

So I took authority in Jesus' name and rebuked it. Anne-Marie started coughing. It left.

That evening, Anne-Marie testified. She had been total-ly healed. For the first time in months, she had been able to kneel down and praise the Lord.

Our God is an awesome God!

36

POWER OF PRAYER
MARSEILLE

I could sense it. I recognised it. It was lurking outside the entrance door to my little apartment in downtown Marseille. I immediately prayed. I was not going to allow this evil spirit to enter. But where did it come from?

My neighbour, Naceera, was a strong believing Christian. She had left her former faith years ago. Her husband was currently travelling, but her cousin was visiting. I went to see her and explained what I sensed. Naceera then asked her cousin if she was reciting her ritualistic prayers in her bedroom. She was, and was politely but firmly requested to stop. What happened next showed me that certain ritualistic prayers are not harmless.

And the battle was on. But not just on the human level.

The next day, I received a desperate phone call. My friend spoke with difficulty. I could hardly understand her words. She needed me to come over immediately. As I walked into her apartment, I was horrified. Her face was swollen and she was struggling to breathe. It seemed as if an invisible hand was strangling her.

I immediately dragged her out of her apartment into mine.

Then I rushed down to fetch another neighbour, also a believer. A demonic force was at work. My friend was gasping for breath. She was suffocating. We prayed and took authority in Jesus' name and the demon let go. Slowly, her breathing became normal again. She was going to be OK.

Needless to say, the cousin was asked to leave. That lady had obviously tapped into the occult, which is not unusual for women from a North African background.

Over the years, I have often seen such attacks and also the power of the name of Jesus against them.

"Our struggle is not against flesh and blood, but against the rulers, against the authorities, against the powers of this dark world and against the spiritual forces of evil in the heavenly realm." (Ephesians 6:12)

37

THE PRETTY FRENCH GIRL

A girl had asked to rent a room in YWAM's hospitality apartment here in Marseille and I had agreed. She only needed the room a few days per week for her studies.

Soon we started talking. She seemed nervous, twisting her fingers. She told me that she was living with a man, but they were not married. She would return every weekend to be with him. She had been a church-goer, the daughter of believing parents. But every church she had gone to had let her know that she was living in sin. So she had stopped going to church.

I immediately felt the Holy Spirit say: "Do not condemn her."

So I listened quietly, waiting for the Holy Spirit to lead the conversation.

"Who is God for you?" I asked.

"He is our Creator... I guess."

"And Jesus, who is He for you personally?"

"I don't really know."

She had never encountered Jesus herself. The relationship with her boyfriend was not the real issue. My heart was filled with compassion for her.

I told her that God was not condemning her and neither

was I. She was surprised, but also relieved. She had been so afraid that I too would accuse her. Then I shared who Jesus was and she listened.

A few days later, she knocked at my door. She had a dream the previous night. In the dream, she had stood at death's door and she knew instantly that she needed to give her life to Jesus. She was still shaking as she walked in.

It was a beautiful birth. Jesus wrapped His arms around her and she wept. She was home, at last.

A few months later she and her boyfriend were married.... in a church!

38

PERFECT LOVE CASTS OUT FEAR

A young lady wanted me to come and visit her family. She had many fears, even though she had given her life to the Lord. Those fears were invading her, stifling her. Her mother had asked if I could come and pray.

After the ceremonial welcome cup of coffee, we wandered off into a bedroom. We wanted some privacy and so we left her father in the living-room.

Violette explained the fears she had. She would wake up afraid and go to bed afraid. She had had these fears all her life. Her mother was concerned. What was wrong? Was it something occult? I did not know, but I sensed the holy presence of God. He knew. We prayed and waited on the Lord. To my surprise, He told me that it was linked with an event in the mother's life.

So I asked her.

"Did something happen when your daughter was born? Something difficult, sad or terrible?"

Her mother stared at me. She had not expected this.

Timidly, nervously she shared. While she was pregnant, her husband was secretly seeing another woman. Violette's mother had been so angry, so hurt. Feelings of rejection, pain, and sorrow had overwhelmed her. Her pregnancy had been a deep, dark walk. I sensed that her emotions at that time had deeply affected her daughter. The little girl was born in sorrow, hurt, pain and anger. She had not been welcomed with joy, as a precious, beautiful treasure. And these emotions had caused deep rejection in her life, leading to constant fear.

The father had since repented and broken off his relationship with his mistress. His wife had forgiven him. But the emotional wounds had scarred little Violette. They needed to be healed and removed.

We prayed. Tears flowed as the Lord ministered deep healing, restoration.

39

SOURAYA

We were walking along the hospital grounds. Suddenly, out of the blue, Souraya spoke out:

"You're different. You have a relationship with God."

Her words were so unexpected, yet so sincere. Yes, indeed, that was a major difference. How did she know? I had not yet said a word about God, about a relationship with Christ. But she was a Muslim and they have a natural inclination to sense things in the spiritual realm.

Soon we were sharing more. She wanted to hear how I had encountered God. I told her stories of people from her general ethnic background who had met Jesus through dreams and visions. She desperately wanted that. But somehow believed it was not possible for her to change her faith.

But as for her little baby girl, that was different. She wanted her to follow my faith and to be baptised. I explained that a conversion came from the heart, that her baby was too young to understand. She was barely a few months old. Souraya was disappointed, so I suggested that her baby girl could be presented to the Lord to be blessed. The idea appealed to Souraya. Yes, so be it. The baby's father was an atheist. He didn't care.

I wondered where to take her as I was visiting another country. I found a church that seemed appropriate and invited Souraya to come with me. It was the first time she attended a church service. I thought she might be intimidated and stay in the back, but she confidently walked up to the front seats. She sat through the service, the songs, the message and enjoyed everything. I did not really know this church but decided I could always approach the American pastor with my strange request.

"Hello, you don't know me. I am a visitor. A friend of mine is here. She is not a Christian, but she would like her baby girl to be presented to Jesus and be blessed. The baby's father is an atheist. What do you think?"

"Sure. Why not? Of course, we can bless the baby."

And they did. I was no longer in that city when it happened, but I can say, without a doubt, that the Lord's hand is upon that little girl today.

As for Souraya, she still waited for her own blessing. She had been taught that she was not allowed to change her faith, even though she desperately wanted to. Eventually, I got her to speak to a friend of mine, a lovely Algerian lady who had encountered Christ. This woman did not hold back. She spoke boldly revealing the true story of her life, the many hurts and pains she had endured in the past and how the amazing love of Jesus had brought deep healing to her soul. Souraya had never heard of such things, and was deeply touched. On that day, she chose Jesus. She too became a follower of Christ.

40

AN ANGEL?

My heart ached as I walked into her hospital room. My mother seemed so frail. It would not be long now.

Somehow I looked at her roommate. That woman seemed in an even worse state. Before I knew it, I was sharing the Gospel with her. I asked her if she wanted to give her life to the Lord. Actually, no, I insisted. I told her that today might be her last chance. She nodded her head and I prayed. I held her hand and my mother's. As I finished the prayer, my mother added a clear amen. I was surprised, pleasantly surprised.

The next day I returned. The bed beside my mother was empty. The woman was gone. I never saw her again. Had she died? I do not know.

Two other ladies were also visiting my mother. We sang a few worship songs with her and then left.

The following day, I came alone. My mother smiled at me.

"Who was this nice young man who came with you yesterday?"

"There was no man with us, mum. We were only three women."

"Oh no. There were four of you. I saw him. Such a wonderful man. Such a lovely smile. He had so much love in his eyes when he looked at me."

"There was no man. What are you talking about?"

"The man dressed in white. He did not speak. But he had such compassion."

A doctor, a nurse?

It took a while before it dawned on me. Had my mother seen an angel? I believe it was Jesus Himself.

It was going to be all right.

41

DISCIPLESHIP MINISTRY

I was in Spain at a YWAM conference. The organisers intro-
duced an American couple to us saying that they were available for counselling. I decided to sign up. I could do with some
prayer.

But when I entered the prayer room, a different couple was
there. I was puzzled, but I stayed and we prayed together. But
why did I feel that I needed to see this other husband and
wife? What was so important?

So I signed up again, this time making sure I was signing up
for the right couple. The next day I went in for the appointment. Only the lady was there. I liked her instantly. We talked
about discipleship, ministry, France and we forgot why I had
come. In the end, she prayed for me. I left feeling that we had
had a great time, but not understanding the *why* of our encounter.

Several months went by. My finances were desperately low.
Someone mentioned translation work, so I decided to accept
it. As soon as the first manual came for translation, my heart
almost missed a beat. The subject was *Hearing God's Voice*, my
favourite, the one that had changed my life. Then I realised
that it was the ministry that the American couple living in

Spain had founded. So that was why we had met in Spain!

I translated and dug into the material. It was good stuff, quality stuff. It was a course for a group setting. Then I distinctly felt the Holy Spirit say: "They will ask you to lead the courses in France." I decided to wait. Two months later, I received a phone call.

"Would you please consider leading and launching the work in France?"

Of course. Pretty soon a small team got together. The international founders came and anointed and appointed me. We were ready. We ran the first course among ourselves.

A few weeks later, as I was walking home, I saw a pastor on the other side of the street. I waved to him. Then felt the Holy Spirit say: "Go and talk to him." So I crossed the street and came up to him. I did not know what I was supposed to talk to him about, so we just chatted. "What are you up to these days?" he asked.

"Oh, translating discipleship material."

"Discipleship material? Tell me more. We need that."

And that's how we started off. We ran the first course there. They were delighted and asked for a second course. We started running more courses. I ended up leading the ministry in France for four years until I handed it over to someone else.

42

"DID YOU SAY DIVORCE?"

"My wife is filing for divorce." He spoke calmly, then looked at us.

We had come together to plan the next discipleship course. It was meant to be a fun time of sharing and preparation. But his comment dropped like a bomb. We stared at him. My fellow co-worker got fidgety. This was not the time to counsel. But as I looked at him, I knew that we needed to listen.

"What happened?"

He shared. It was so unexpected, but his wife was determined to divorce. She wanted to keep the house. Their 18 year-old twins, a boy and a girl, would stay with her. Neither the wife nor the children attended church nor did they want to.

Then this sudden thought flashed through my mind. When it's that sudden and unexpected, I know it's from God, not from me. The thought was: "Send the visiting YWAM team into his home." So I asked him and he immediately said yes.

Then I asked the YWAM team and, of course, they said yes too.

A few days later we arrived. As soon as we entered the house I noticed the silence. No-one was there to greet us. There was a heaviness in the air. I could tell that the father was upstairs trying to coax his family to come into the living room.

I prayed silently, but deep inside I just knew that God was in total control. No need to fret. The Lord was going to do the work. Finally, the daughter came down and promptly sat right in the middle of the group of young YWAMers. There was no fear, no shyness. The mother also arrived but sat in a corner. She was not happy. But the young daughter listened intently as the YWAM team sang worship songs and shared their testimonies. The Lord was clearly opening her ears and her heart.

When they finished, she sat there, waiting... for something to happen. So I asked her:

"Have you ever given your life to Jesus?"

"I tried."

"Would you like to try again, now?"

"Yes!" It was loud and clear.

I asked a young fiery evangelist in the YWAM team to lead her into the kingdom of God and Louna was born again! She spent the rest of the evening hanging out with the team. Laughter filled the once gloomy house.

The divorce came to a standstill. The daughter no longer wanted her father to leave. The mother did not know what to do as this was not what she had planned. So husband and wife decided to work it through. They were reconciled and the divorce case was dropped. Today they are happily married.

43

THE GARDEN

It is peaceful this morning. I am sitting in a comfortable armchair, looking out of the window. I see only the green of trees. It is hot outside, but there is a gentle breeze blowing through the house, keeping me nice and cool.

Green is such a peaceful colour. It soothes our soul. God, as ever, has done the right thing. I'm so glad he didn't choose to make leaves black or grey or …. Colours are important. God knew, from the beginning, that we would need peace for our souls.

And today, as I have time to reflect, I realise that His plans for us were good from the very beginning. God intended for us to live in a garden. A garden, where we can walk in the cool of the evening and enjoy the few sounds of life around us, the scurrying of small creatures, the smell of trees, plants, flowers... the sight of the moon and the stars shining brightly. God wanted us to live in a garden... His intentions were good. He is concerned not only for our spirit but also our soul and body.

Psalm 23 took on a new meaning for me today:
He makes me lie down in green pastures
He leads me beside still waters
He restores my soul.

It is good to pray for one another, it is wonderful to have counsellors advise you when you are feeling down. But sometimes all we need is to lie down in green pastures in order to be restored in our soul. And a restored soul brings joy to the spirit.

44

PRECIOUS PRODUCT

I was in deep thought this morning.

Several years ago, there was a real need in France. Those of us working here knew that and we knew that the help could come from only one country... America!

So when we heard of visiting Americans coming, there was always a mad scramble as we all rushed to make phone calls, send emails, and place orders for this much coveted product: peanut butter.

Yes, we were serving in the land of the world's best gourmet cooks, the finest wines, cheeses, and baguettes. But the need for peanut butter was there. It could not be found in any shops, supermarkets or elsewhere. We were desperate. So we waited with much anxiety for our visitors from America. And those brave Americans sacrificially obliged, lugging jars of peanut butter through airports, on trains, buses, cars. They would not rest until they had delivered the treasured product to us, relieving us till the jars were once again empty.

Well, nowadays, France has changed. Peanut butter can be found almost anywhere and today, as I looked at my jar of peanut butter, I was reminded of all the stress and anxiety that this product has inflicted upon so many of us. And I suddenly realised with a thankful heart that a great stress factor has been lifted off my shoulders.

Anyway, I just wanted you all to know that I am very thankful today.

Cordula
August 2014

45

NOURIA

I was attending a gathering of a national house-church net-work in France where I had the privilege of running three workshops on understanding the faith of the Muslim people. There were ten participants.

It was a joy to teach this group because there was a real determination to understand, not just plain curiosity. They wanted to know. They were taking notes. They were asking questions. They were praying. They want to be used by God to reach out to these people, to make a difference, to not remain passive. There was a sense of urgency.

Just as I was about to start, an Algerian lady, Nouria, walked into the room. "I don't know why I am here. I don't need this teaching because of my background. But the Holy Spirit told me to come."

I always begin my first teaching by explaining the very foundations of Islam. It is crucial to understand the origins, other-wise, we could be misled to thinking that it is just another re-ligion created by man. It is not. There are spiritual forces at the very roots. As I shared, Nouria gasped. She had never heard that. It was too much for her and she ran out of the room. She came back at the end of the meeting. She was devastated. "I did not know. I did not know."

The second day, I shared on world-view and it included talking about the status of women. I have heard so many heartbreaking stories of Muslim women. I shared some of them. Nouria burst into tears and once again ran out of the room. Later on, we met and she told me what had happened. The Holy Spirit had revealed deep hurts from her past, things she had forgotten, or rather suppressed.

As a very young teenager she had been sexually assaulted by a family member. She had run to her mother for help, for comfort. But her mother had beaten her. Why? Because sexual assault is a shameful thing for the family. Why is it shameful? Because it is commonly believed that it is the girl's fault. So Nouria was assaulted again, and again, and no one helped. She had never understood why no-one helped. She had felt vulnerable, alone, and hurt.

But this week she understood. She was able to forgive and I could pray for her. I know that the Lord Jesus is now healing her heart.

46

THE CRY FOR COMPASSION
AND THE CALL FOR CAUTION

January 2016, Marseille. (Written shortly after the terrorist attacks in Paris.)

I think I must have slept through something here. As I walked down Marseille's main shopping street the other day, I noticed that almost 90 % (yes!) of the population in this area is North African. I have never seen so many veiled women around. There are more and more bearded men with their long oriental robes too, huddled together, talking. What happened?

Actually, I think I am only noticing it because I just came back from a very western environment in the USA. I needed the contrast to understand what is going on in my city. Or rather, in my part of the city, where the economic situation is dire. There are, of course, other beautiful quarters in Marseille where the middle and upper class population reside. And then, there is the Mediterranean Sea with its stunning beaches.

Yet despite the financial hardships in my neighbourhood, I have never met so many overly friendly people. They go out of their way to be polite. They let you go ahead of them to the cashier and apologise if they accidentally bump into you. They are quick to pick up something you may have dropped and often smile at you. I think they may be afraid you could think that they too are involved in terrorism.

In the light of many terrorist attacks that have happened in Paris, California, and Cologne, it is crucial that the Church knows what we are dealing with.

I hear two opposing voices in Europe, both within the Church and in the world: the *"Cry for Compassion"* and the *"Call to be Cautious."* My answer to both is : Yes!

Yes, we need to reach out to refugees who are in need. We can share the love of Jesus, both practically and by preaching the Gospel message. We can ask the Holy Spirit to lead us to those who are truly searching.

But we must know that Islam is not just a religion. It is also a worldview which affects all spheres of society. It is territorial and it is undergirded by spiritual forces. We need to also understand that most Muslims are not overly concerned about this. Their lives revolve around their homes, jobs, and children. Like all of us, they seek acceptance and friendship, and it is our privilege to be able to reach out to them.

Some of the best things we can do against fanaticism are to pray for the protection of our police, wisdom for our governments, and to reach out in Christian hospitality to cultures and religions that are different from our own. We can ask God to touch the Muslim people, that they too would personally encounter Jesus, who truly loves them. May they receive supernatural dreams and visions of Christ as they seek truth for their lives.

47

THE BEAUTIFUL BLUE DRESS

I have learnt a lot this week. Yesterday was particularly interesting.

We had gone to a colleague's farewell, a missionary going-home party in her local church. It was in a very North African area of town. The main street, side-streets, the mosque, the shops, the housing complexes...

Towards the end of the evening, I asked Paul, a brother in Christ, if he could give me a ride home.

So three of us, Paul, another lady and I started to walk towards his car. He had parked it in one of the many side-streets. As we walked along, I had an uncanny feeling. A couple of young men brushed past us. We were in a dark alley. The pavement was so small that we could not walk alongside one another. I was the last one in line. Suddenly, I heard "Madam, madam". At first, it sounded like the typical: "Madam, please give me a Euro." But there was something nasty about this call. A young man rushed past me and swung about. He pointed a knife at me. The blade was about 20 cms (approx. 8 inches) long. It looked like a hunting knife. He demanded that I give him my handbag.

The knife was only a few inches from my dress. My beautiful

blue dress. I realised, with horror, that the knife would rip it. I immediately yelled at him. "How dare you!" Fear was not on my mind, only anger and concern for my beautiful dress.

As soon as he heard me, Paul whipped ground and grabbed the young man by the throat.

At the same time, I felt someone from behind pull violently at my handbag, which I always carry strapped diagonally across my back (*which is a must in Marseille*). I never carry credit or debit cards, checks or much money with me (*also a must in Marseille*). But I did have my health insurance card and my house-keys. I wasn't going to give them up. So we struggled. For some reason, the guy quickly gave up and rushed to help his colleague who was fighting with Paul.

All the shouting had brought neighbouring North Africans out on the street. They immediately yelled at the thieves, who ran off, but unfortunately, the men had the time to rob Paul of his small pouch which carried his ID card and other papers. The North Africans who had rescued us crowded around us. They were obviously upset. They seemed ashamed that some of their people had robbed us. Having them around was good.

It was an eventful evening. I was so happy that my beautiful blue dress had not been damaged.

Oh, and Paul's bag was found the next day. Apart from a few coins, everything else was still in his bag.

48

THE GOLDEN RETRIEVER

It was summer, 2016, and I was in the Pyrenees, France. Friends had very kindly invited me to spend a week with them in a pretty chalet high up in the mountains. There were seven of us.

One day, we went to a lake. The scenery was beautiful. The lake was surrounded by mountains. People were laying around in the sun, reading, chatting, sometimes laughing, but all in quiet tones. There was no shouting, no yelling into a phone, no one screaming at their kids or dogs. Everything was peaceful. I realised I was going through culture shock. I was no longer in downtown Marseille.....

And then I saw her, this beautiful golden retriever. She came charging down the slopes and went straight for the lake. It was obvious that she had set her heart on a swim. But just an inch away from the water, she stopped in her tracks, swung around and stared at something in the distance. I realised she waited for her master's command. But the master did not come. I felt sorry for her. She pranced around on all fours, desperate for a swim. I tried to coax her to go into the water. But she did not budge, she did not even look at me. Her eyes looked straight at her master, or rather mistress. And then the mistress came.

One look, a smile that gave permission, and the golden retriever pounced into the water. For the rest of the afternoon, she was the happiest dog around, much to everybody else's delight. Several swimmers would approach her, trying to play with her, but she obeyed only her mistress and the children who were obviously part of the family. She was focused.

I will never forget that look, a look of total obedience, devotion to her mistress. And it reminded me of how we should be in our walk as disciples. We are to focus on Jesus, obeying His commands and not letting the enemy entice or coax us into doing something without the Lord's permission. He is our master and He is a good master.

49

CHEAP COFFINS

It was Christmas time. December 2016. There were no strikes. Generally, around this time of the year, there are a variety of strikes in France. It could be a train strike, an airport strike, pilots, traffic control personnel, baggage claims or whatever. But this year they only went on strike in Paris, so I quickly jumped on a low-cost airplane bound for Berlin.

The plane was small and packed. I don't know what it was made of, but we rock'n rolled our way to Berlin. Shortly before landing, the pilot made an announcement. His voice was very calm. He told us not to be alarmed, but that we would land a bit away from the regular runway. The plane had been losing some type of liquid. For security reasons, he needed to make sure that everything was OK. He had requested the arrival of fire engines. No reason to get alarmed, he said. Just standard procedure. He spoke very confidently. So, of course, nobody got alarmed.

As soon as we landed, fire engines surrounded the plane. My neighbour suddenly said :"Have you noticed that we are very, very far away from the airport building and far from any other plane ?"

I realised he was right. "Yes, I guess it's in the event that we blow up." Now, I have this strange ability to remain calm when things get dangerous. So, as I sat there, the thought occurred to me that there is always a bright side to whatever happens. I suddenly realised that, in the event of an explosion (and ensuing death), the airline would have to cover my burial costs. It made me feel strangely relieved.

But then, of course, we never did explode. The plane eventually taxied off, fire engines still following us, and quietly parked. We all got off and I switched my thoughts back to Christmas.

Upon my return to Marseille, however, somehow the subject of burial cropped up again. I wondered why coffins cost so much. Did the wood really have to be so expensive, the lining so fancy? It seemed like a big money business. So, for a few weeks, I toyed with the idea of starting a business selling cheap coffins. It would be so helpful, I thought, until I found out that someone else had had the same brilliant idea. So I dropped those thoughts and focused on missions again.

50

THE JOYFUL WIDOW

Her name was Messaouda. She was living in a women's shelter in Marseille, where I served in the chaplaincy. She was a smiling, bubbly lady. I was intrigued. All the other women were always complaining about their dire circumstances. So I asked her: "Messaouda, what makes you so happy?" "Oh," she said with a smile, "I am so happy because my husband died."

Now, Messaouda was Algerian and I knew that often North African men are taught to consider women as inferior in mind, spirit, and soul. Also, the women must not be seen, lest they seduce men and thus damage the husband's honour. So they must be veiled in order to protect their husband's reputation. Some of them, like Messaouda, are actually not even allowed out of the house.

Messaouda had been locked in her apartment for 25 years. Her husband forbade her to leave. She had no children, so her days were solitary. Except on those very, very rare occasions when her husband was sick, too sick to go shopping. Then she was allowed out, but only to the bakery across the street and only for a few minutes. Messaouda told me those few minutes were the highlights of her life. She would stand in line at the bakery waiting for her turn, listening to voices, seeing other faces. Often, she would let other people take her turn. Anything to stay a little longer. The thrill, the joy of being alive!

When her husband died, Messaouda opened the door and left the apartment. She wandered down the street, saw a coffee shop, pulled out a chair and sat down. She ordered a coffee and smiled. She was free!

I asked her what her next plan was.

"Will you return to your home country?"

"Never. Someone in my enlarged family will marry me off again. I will stay here. My next plan is to buy a metro/subway ticket and travel through the city of Marseille, and just observe, enjoy and live!"

Yes, I have met a joyful widow.

PS: Messaouda's situation is rare. She was married to a particularly strict fundamentalist. Of course, not all Muslim men lock up their wives like that.

51

THE BEGGAR AND THE COAT

The Bible clearly tells us that we are to give to those who ask, to those who are in need. What exactly does that mean?

I used to live in a neighbourhood where there were at least ten beggars on my street. Gypsy ladies in their long bright skirts, carrying babies in their arms, their toddlers playing with empty beer bottles or whatever else they picked up on the dirty streets, for lack of toys. My heart went out to them. You give a little one a teddy bear and the next day he no longer has it. Where has it gone?

Other beggars, and alcoholics, drug addicts, and prostitutes. So many needs.

Each and every one of them asks for money. I did some mental calculating. If I were to give to every beggar I meet every day, then pretty soon, I too would be sitting on the streets and begging! Was that God's will for me? Was I to give to the point of making myself destitute as well? I decided that it was not God's will. But I am to give, as He leads, as He indicates, to the person He chooses on that particular day, in that specific situation.

Then one morning, while I was at home, I heard Him speak: "I want you to give away one of your coats today."

It was unexpected, as is often the case when God speaks.

I had two coats. I did not mind. One was enough. The morning led to early afternoon. I forgot about the coats. Sometime later, I had to run out for an errand. It was winter. I pulled on my coat and went out. As I stepped out into the cold, I noticed a beggar woman standing nearby. I mumbled a short *hello* and continued my walk. Something made me stop. Did she need anything? A coin, a piece of bread? I went back to her.

"Do you need something?"

"I am so cold," she whispered. I had not noticed before. She had no coat. It was indeed very cold. I grabbed her by the arm and shoved her into the doorway of our apartment building. I quickly pulled off my coat and gave it to her. She burst into tears. She was overwhelmed with gratitude and I have to admit that I too was overwhelmed by the fact that God had spoken so specifically. He had known, all along, what this woman needed.

Shortly afterwards, someone offered me a coat. Then another one. And another one. And only recently, many years later, someone called me.

"I have a brand new coat. I have never used it. I would like to give it to you. I think it will fit you."

It did. It was perfect. I love it.

52

BAPTISM IN THE CALANQUES

Remember Acts 8, the story of Philip, this wild evangelist and his encounter with the Ethiopian? Well, this is the 21st century version of this story. Read on.

It is the story of a young lady from Germany. Her longing and desire to know more about God brought her all the way to France. She asked to serve as a volunteer with a travelling YWAM team and was accepted. As she moved around with them, they taught her. And then they came to Marseille. The team asked me to come and teach them on how to share the Gospel with our *cousins* (Muslims). So I spent a full afternoon with them, teaching and answering many questions. We had a great time together.

But that was not the best part. It happened during the break. This young lady came up to me and said: "I want to have an encounter with Jesus." She was ready. Somehow, ironically, the teaching on the differences between Islam and Christianity had finalised her decision. Her heart's desire was to pray and give her life to the Lord in her mother tongue, German. I was so amazed at God's incredible organising of events. He sent her to France, then down to Marseille, arranged for us to meet, and, of course, I could pray with her in German. And so she entered into the kingdom of God right then and there.

And the story goes on. Do you remember that the Ethiopian said to Philip: "Look, here is water. Why shouldn't I be baptised?" A few days later I explained to this young lady that she needed to consider water baptism and she said: "Why shouldn't I be baptised here and now, in the Mediterranean?" So, we asked her to get her parents' blessing, which she did.

For a short while, we wondered about church politics. You see, it was 2015, in France. Very many churches still believe that only a pastor should baptise. She was due to leave in a few days. She knew no pastor in this city, but she definitely wanted to be baptised. So we did it.

We drove to one of the magnificent coves (called the Calanques) in the Mediterranean. It was cold, but it was beautiful. She couldn't wait. She was as pretty as a bride. The water was freezing, but she was determined. We got into the ice-cold water and baptised her.

As she came out, she exclaimed: "Look, a rainbow! A sign for me!"

It was a delightful day! In heaven and on earth.

53

OUTREACH IN A MARSEILLE CHURCH
2015

I was chatting with an evangelical pastor and suddenly asked him if he wanted to invite a YWAM team to his church. He hesitated because he had heard that YWAM moves in the gifts of the Holy Spirit. His church was not too familiar with that. But he had also heard that YWAM was passionate about Jesus. I suggested that he think about it. The following week I saw him again and asked: "Have you thought about it?" and he said "Not yet." This went on several more times. Finally, I went up to him and said: "You need to take a risk. If not for a Sunday morning, why not invite us for an evening meeting?" He took a deep breath and said: Yes!

So we arrived. There were about 20 people from the church. The YWAM team from California did a great job leading worship, giving testimonies. They spoke with passion. The pastor was beaming. But this was just the beginning. After the performance, one of the American ladies felt led to speak to a young French lady. So we walked up to her. As soon as we approached her, tears welled up in her eyes. Something was bothering her. So we asked her if she had given her life to Jesus and she said yes, she had done so silently in her heart.

"Did you speak it out loud? Did you confess with your mouth? Did you tell Jesus that you want to walk with him?" I enquired.

She had never heard this. No one had ever told her. So, right then and there she prayed and the Lord turned on His shower of love and poured it all over her. She wept and wept. The pastor's young daughter and son were right there, witnessing it all. They were amazed. They had never experienced something like this. The pastor came up almost leaping for joy.

And there were others, like this woman who wanted prayer because she had fears. When I asked if she had been filled with the Holy Spirit, she gave me this incredible reply: "No, I am afraid of the Holy Spirit because He is holy and if I'm not holy, He will get mad with me." Two young men from the YWAM team gave her a beautiful explanation of the Holy Spirit while I translated for them. Then she overcame her fear and prayed and asked the Holy Spirit to fill her and He gently, very, very gently touched her heart.

And in the end, I made a diplomatic mistake. I asked the pastor if the young YWAM team could pray for him. He said yes and the team said yes and I forgot to tell them that he is not used to the laying on of hands and prophecies etc. And, of course, a young 20-year old laid hands on him and prayed and blessed him and another one prophesied over him. But he was beaming, smiling. So I guess it wasn't an error after all.

It was a good day.

54

MAMA DUCK

Back to Marseille and the house-church...

We held our first *outdoor* service. We went to a park near the beach and it was beautiful, sitting on a blanket and worshipping, despite rumba background music from another group.

While we waited for everyone to gather, I watched a mama duck and her 12 ducklings swim by. Something that looked like an otter was splashing around. Then a sea gull swooped down and grabbed something from the lake. On the bank, a little field rat scuttled by. Kind of cute, even though the others didn't think so.

At the end of the service, I wandered towards the lake, wondering how on earth a mama duck can take care of 12 little ones at the same time. Can you imagine?

The ducklings were swimming peacefully. Mama was nowhere in sight. Little did I know that two of her young ones were happily exploring the shore where I was headed. As I got closer, there was a sudden loud skidding sound, Mama duck had landed on the water and let out a very authoritarian *quack.*

Within a split second, the two ducklings hurtled towards her, their little wings flapping wildly. I realised I had almost trodden on them. But Mama duck was there and had been watching.

And I got my answer. It is the voice of authority and obedience that helps her keep her ducklings in line. It reminded me of how God deals with us. We can't see Him, but He sees us and watches over us, even when we are wandering off and putting ourselves in danger. Are we as obedient as the two little ducklings?

55

THE MAN FROM TEL AVIV

April 2017. We had just finished a very fulfilling two days at the YWAM Provence base, here in France. It had been a joy to reconnect, pray together, listen to God, and also have fun.

I hopped on the train heading back to Marseille. It was one of those old trains. You know, the ones with compartments and sliding doors for privacy that can seat eight people. They always remind me of the film *Murder on the Orient Express.* Anyway, I found a seat and settled down. If there's one thing I love doing when traveling by train, it's *nothing!* I love staring out at the countryside, without really seeing anything. My mind switches off. I'm on pause. I find it so refreshing and relaxing.

There was only one other man in that compartment. He seemed fidgety, restless. He shuffled around and changed seats a couple of times. I looked at him out of the corner of my eye. He seemed worried, anxious. Something was obviously bothering him. I immediately sensed that my train ride was not going to be a very quiet trip. So I had the usual spirit and flesh conversation. My flesh said: "Ignore him and relax." My spirit said: "Talk to him!" Well, the man started talking to me.

He was French but lived abroad. He was searching for a new

location to resettle in France. Could I recommend a town or a city? I asked him where he lived now. "Tel Aviv, Israel." That triggered my attention. So I asked him the obvious question: "Are you a Jew?" He was.

"Are you a believer?" No, he didn't believe in God, only in some remote superior force.

I couldn't help but tell him: "Sir, I think you're looking for God, not a location." To my surprise, he was not upset.

"Have you read the Torah?" No, he had tried once but found it too complicated.

"How about the Gospels?" No, there are four of them, right? He'd heard of them.

I challenged him to try reading them one day. He listened.

Another question. I like using questions because they cause people to reflect and often they get their own revelation during the conversation.

"Have you ever prayed?" No. Not really. Well... He did pray the Jewish prayer every morning.

"So, you do believe?" I asked. He smiled.

"Have you ever just talked to God, like a very personal prayer?" No. He never had. But suddenly his eyes lit up. He moved closer towards me. "Yes, yes," he said emphatically. He had once lost his wallet and had cried out: "God, if you exist, help me!" And his prayer had been answered.

"So, there you go. God exists." I said. "He knows you, cares for you and answers your prayers." The man was smiling now. He nodded his head. He started talking very fast. He became excited as the realisation hit him. He had experienced God. The train slowed down and came to a standstill. We had arrived at his station. Eyes shining, the man from Tel Aviv nimbly jumped off the train. A searching man had come one step closer to God.

56

THE STORY OF THE OLIVE TREE

Some time ago, I was in Malaga, Spain, and a friend told me that the Lord had once spoken to him under an olive tree concerning a very important question. This somehow triggered my interest. After his departure, I wandered around looking for one. There were loads of them. I finally found a tree that looked like it had a certain anointing and sat under it, in vain. God did not speak...

But I did have a small olive tree on my terrace in Marseille. I had rescued it from a neighbour. Every time I went down to visit this person, I would notice this poor withered olive tree or rather bush. I finally told her that I was going to sue her for plant mistreatment. She very reluctantly admitted that I was right. And so the little olive bush wandered up onto my terrace, where it received intensive care. Soon more leaves started growing. But I also knew that the day would come when I would have to get it out of its Roman amphora type jar and re-pot it into a larger one.

Now, generally, re-potting is pretty straightforward, right? It only takes a few minutes. Move a plant from one pot over into the next one. Not this one. Because the opening of the amphora was smaller than the rest of the jar, I had to literally hand spoon out the earth, then wrench and pull, and wrench and pull. When I finally got the olive bush out, I was aghast: it had thousands of little roots rolled around in circles, desperate for more soil. And, as I stood there, holding this suffocating plant, the Lord spoke to me: "This is just like you, you are in a place where you can no longer grow. You need more space." (Both spiritually and geographically.)

I carefully placed the olive-tree into its slightly bigger pot, wondering if it would survive after such rough treatment.

Then my friend Maria, from Wisconsin, USA, came to visit me. She wandered in with her usual smile and said she had been praying and received the following verse for me from Psalm 52:8: "But I am like an olive tree flourishing in the house of God..."

She had no idea that I had developed a sudden interest in these trees. This, of course, caused me to look up the meaning in the Bible. I found out that olive trees were the most honoured, valued, cherished trees in the Old Testament, used for a variety of spiritual purposes (in the temple, for the anointing of kings, etc.).

This awesome new revelation made me run out and check on my bush. To my great surprise, three little olives were there! Wow, it was bearing fruit. But only a bit of fruit. I knew that it would have to be planted into a garden, where it would be able to fully stretch out its roots and grow. And the Lord spoke to me again. "You will also move twice. First a larger apartment, and then there will be an even bigger move."

And that's how I had total peace about moving into my friend's larger apartment here in Marseille.

57

OLIVIA'S RESCUE

My little olive bush now has a name: Olivia.

Well, last night we smuggled her out of my housing block. Soon she will be replanted into a garden and enter into her God-ordained destiny to spread her roots and become a flourishing tree.

I wrote *smuggled her out* because my neighbour found out that I was moving. She called me up and told me that all of her other plants had pitifully withered to death under the scorching summer sun in Marseille, for lack of care and water. She told me she wanted Olivia back, but I told her that Olivia was destined to a much higher calling than to wither on her terrace. So our relationship slightly deteriorated. My friend, JP, came that very night and carried her out. He carefully placed her on the sidewalk and left to fetch his car. To my distress, he had placed her under a bright street lamp. I quickly shoved Olivia into a darker corner while stealthily looking over my shoulder in case my neighbour strolled by.

While this was happening I realised that I was definitely entering into a very different season of my life. For several years I had smuggled Bibles into a closed country. We would walk through customs trying very hard to look relaxed and even harder not to smile when they waved us past. Then we would make the long drive up the mountains. Every so often, some terrorists would set up road blocks, forcing cars to stop and then proceeded to cut peoples' throats. I don't smuggle Bibles there anymore. The Church in that country now has a printing press and internet access as well. I soberly realised that I had downgraded to smuggling olive trees!

The neighbour never strolled by. I waved good-bye to JP and Olivia and went home. As I walked into my hallway I noticed a small olive on the floor. It must have fallen off when JP carried her out. I picked it up and decided to keep it as a reminder of what God had told me: that I too was destined to become a flourishing olive tree.

Oh, by the way, my neighbour and I are friends again.

58

THE SUN, THE SEA, AND THE YOUNG MAN

I was lying on the beach, enjoying the sun and the beautiful Mediterranean Sea. Suddenly, I noticed this handsome young man stroll down towards the water. He was the healthy, sporty type. I immediately thought: "He's probably ever so vain and selfish because of his great looks."

The young man dropped a couple of towels and other beach equipment on the sand, then walked back towards his car. I saw him help an elderly man out of the car. He picked him up and carried him towards the water, followed by a little 2 or 3-year-old boy. Prancing alongside them was a Labrador puppy. The young man carefully settled the older man, maybe his grandpa, onto the towel. All the while, he kept a close watch on the little boy.

He then spent the rest of the afternoon with the boy, holding him as he splashed in the water or playing with him in the sand. On and off he would chat with "grandpa." At one point, both the older man and the little boy were peacefully lying on their towels. The young man sat down. I suspected that he was looking forward to a moment's rest, except that the little Labrador puppy now claimed his attention. He wanted to play. Without a grumble the man got up and starting throwing him a ball, still keeping an eye on the boy and grandpa. He never rested, never took time for himself and didn't even go for a swim to cool off.

After some hours, he carefully carried a contented old man back to the car, followed by a cheerful boy and a joyful puppy. He had given them all a lovely time at the beach. He was the kindest, most unselfish young man I had ever seen. I was deeply ashamed of my judgemental attitude.

59

HOW OLD AM I, SERIOUSLY?

I hopped onto the bus. It was packed. No seats were available. Almost immediately, a young lady jumped up.

"Please, take my seat."

I stared at her. This had never happened to me before.

"It's OK. I can stand."

She insisted. So I sat down and wondered. Was I really this old? Was this sign of respect good or bad news?

A few days later, I caught the same bus back home. There were some free seats, so I sat down. Slowly the bus filled up. People came in and soon many of them were standing. I was thankful I had a seat.

I then had this strange feeling that someone was staring at me. I looked up and sure enough, three elderly people were staring at me. Or rather, no, they were glaring at me. I wondered why. Slowly it occurred to me that they were coveting my seat. I offered to stand up and immediately one of the elder men shuffled toward me. He mumbled something under his breath, but I heard him.

"No respect for elders nowadays. Hmmmh..."

Both incidents happened that same week.

I realised I was a junior for the seniors and a senior for the juniors.

60

THE STORY OF THE ANTS

I saw them crawling along the kitchen counter and suddenly wondered.

How did God do it? They had mouths, obviously. They were searching for food. But then they must have stomachs and most likely a little heart. How did God manage to squeeze all that into such tiny bodies?

Then I noticed several of them trying to haul the tiniest piece of bread along the counter. They were struggling. It was teamwork. But it seemed like an impossible task. Upon a sudden impulse, I decided to give them a helping hand. My finger moved down towards them. I planned to break the scrap of bread into even smaller pieces so that they could carry it more easily. But as my finger approached them, the ants scrambled away in panic. They were terrified.

I was frustrated. How silly of them. I meant no harm. But I realised it was pointless. They would never understand, not unless I were miraculously transformed into an ant. Then I could reassure them, explain to them that the huge finger meant them no harm. On the contrary, it was intent on blessing them.

And then I remembered that an evangelist had once likened

the story of the ants to Jesus' coming on the earth. Jesus came down as a human being. He walked on earth as a man, pointing towards the Father. Had He come as God, we too would have panicked. We too would have run away. However, as a man, He could walk in our midst to teach us, heal us, deliver us and then die for us.

But then I was glad that I did not have the miraculous power to transform myself into an ant. I do not think I would enjoy walking across a kitchen counter. I am so glad that I have limited abilities.

61

STUNNINGLY BEAUTIFUL

I like plants. But not this one. The leaves were ugly, nothing attractive about them. Why keep it? I made a mental note to get rid of that horrible plant as soon as possible. Tomorrow. But then tomorrow went by, and another day too. For some reason, every day I somehow got sidetracked.

Then one morning, as I stared out of the kitchen window, I gasped. My ugly plant had just sprouted. A beautiful pink flower was blossoming. In fact, it was stunningly beautiful! The next day, there was another flower, just as pretty. And then another one, and another one. Seven pink flowers blossomed in front of my very eyes. They seemed to smile. They were happy to be alive. I was deeply distressed. To think I had planned on throwing this plant away! I would never have enjoyed such a delightful sight. I would have missed out on something of great value.

And then I felt the Lord speak to me. How often do we overlook people? We walk past them. They seem unattractive. Not that they have no value. Every person has value. Every person is precious. But we do not see them.

But if we take the time to stop, to get to know them, then we discover their hidden qualities, their talents, their personalities. In the end, we realise that it was a blessing to get to know them. Maybe it took time, patience, maybe even help and counsel. But the wait would have been worthwhile.

And I am so thankful for the many people who patiently walked alongside me. Maybe they too at first thought I was not worth walking with, but they chose to get to know me and it helped me blossom. It helped me discover myself, to feel my worth, to smile, to be happy to be alive.

That pretty plant was a life lesson for me.

62

ANOTHER BAPTISM
JUNE 2018

Today Sabrina got baptised. Last week she had given her life to Jesus. She was Algerian, from a particular people group. Now she wanted to be baptised. She did not want to wait. But she wanted no photos, no crowds, only her friend and myself. It was not the time to let her family know about her choice. Not yet. They would not understand.

She arrived quite late. When she got there, she told me about this incredible encounter she had just had. On her way, she had *accidentally* bumped into an acquaintance. They had met several times before. But today, of all days, this woman told her that she was an evangelical Christian. And she also told Sabrina to get baptised. Sabrina was amazed. She had not told her that she was on her way to go and get baptised. A holy *coincidence*?!

And all the while I had been wondering if I really should baptise her that soon. After that, I no longer wondered.

I showed her the confession of faith. I wanted to make sure she really understood because she came from such a different spiritual background. She read it out loud and spoke firmly: "Yes. I agree. I understand. I am determined. I want to be baptised."

She had never seen a baptism before. So I explained what we would do in the water. Then off we went to the beach. Sabrina was happy.

"Look. I bought a brand new bikini for the baptism. Isn't it beautiful?"

"Oh..." I replied because I didn't know what else to say.

"You don't think it's a good idea to get a new bikini for a new beginning?" She was puzzled.

"Yes. Yes. Very nice thought. New clothes for a new life." I figured Jesus probably didn't mind, so why should I.

And so Sabrina was baptised... in her brand new bikini!

63

THE COUCH

I fumbled around on my phone, looking at adds on a web-site for a second-hand couch. Then I saw one. Somehow I was drawn to it like a magnet. I clicked on it. A few minutes later I got a response and communicated with the seller. I liked her.

I called my friend, Joëlle. "Want to go check out a couch?"
"Sure."

A few minutes later we were on our way. This could be the couch I was looking for. But I also looked forward to meeting the owner. I didn't know why.

I rang the bell and a pretty, North African girl opened the door. She seemed so young. I liked her instantly. We followed her into her tiny apartment. She had a little boy. I looked at the couch, but it wasn't quite what I wanted. I could, however, feel God's love for this woman. She seemed so vulnerable and fragile, so much in need of protection.

"I'm selling everything because I am leaving Marseille."

"It is good for you to leave Marseille. You will start afresh elsewhere." I don't even know why I said that.

She looked at me. "I am leaving because my husband was violent. I want to forget."

So that was it. I had to tell her. "God loves you so much."

She stared directly into my eyes. "No-one has ever said this to me." Then, a timid smile. "Do you really believe that God loves... me?" She looked for my response, hopefully, expectantly.

"Yes. Absolutely. And He also knows you, in fact, He's known you ever since you were born."

"I know that He knows me. He is God. But I did not know that He also loves me."

So we talked. She was a Muslim. I asked if I could pray a blessing on her in the name of Jesus.

"Yes, of course." So we did. Her little boy suddenly got very noisy. But pretty Linda just listened, spellbound. When we finished praying, she stared at us. A beautiful smile. Shining eyes.

"No-one has ever prayed for me before... has ever told me that God loves me and cares for me. It is almost... almost... as if God ordained this visit. The couch was just an excuse. Could it be?"

Yes, dear Linda, the couch was just an excuse.

It was time to leave. She had received two powerful revelations; that God loved her and that He had specifically sent two people to pray for her. It was enough for the day. She would meet Jesus, one day. He was waiting for her.

64

MOTHER AND DAUGHTER DAY

Another beautiful baptism and it almost didn't happen.

I woke up that Saturday with a heavy heart. Various administrative hurdles to overcome. My gift is not administration and paperwork. I felt submerged with the issues to sort out. But I had promised to baptise a lady. A friend picked me up and off we went. But believe me, I was not in the mood to baptise, to pray or to celebrate.

When we arrived however, it was evident that this lady had been born again. She loved Jesus, loved reading the Bible. She shared how Jesus had already changed her life and had gotten rid of various occult objects in her house. She no longer wanted to wear the dark clothes she used to like. Now she wanted bright, cheerful colours.

I then proceeded to explain about water baptism. She listened intently. Yes, she wanted just that. I also shared about the baptism of the Holy Spirit. Yes, that too. So off to the pool we went.

A delightful baptism followed. One of my best so far. She overcame her fear of ducking her head under water; and when she came out she exclaimed: "What is happening? This is amazing. I am being filled through and through. I am about to burst for joy!" Hugs and kisses followed.

And then I noticed her 9-year-old daughter who had been watching. My heart was filled with compassion for her. Her father had abandoned them several months ago. He rarely came to see her. This little girl was hurting. I asked if I could pray for her.

"My daughter is so shy. I do not think that she will be willing."

"Let's try anyway."

To our surprise, the little girl immediately said "yes." We sat down near the pool and talked. I really just wanted to pray a blessing over her, but before I knew it, I was sharing the Gospel message with her.

She was already reading the Bible. Yes, she knew about Jesus. She wanted Jesus in her life... and became born again. Such a sweet Mother and Daughter day.

And my own frustrations were turned to joy.

65

A FEW KEYS TO HEARING GOD'S VOICE

By now, some of you may be thinking that I always hear God's voice. Not so. It has been a learning process and sometimes it still is.

On my first day at the YWAM base in Austria in the 1980s, a young lady came up to me. After a brief conversation, she said:

"Let's ask God what He thinks about the situation."

I thought she was slightly insane. She really expected God to give her a clear answer. I was so stunned that I don't really remember what else happened. But it was the beginning of my own walk of learning to hear and obey God's voice.

So, how does God talk to us? Good question. The truth is that God created us in order to have a relationship with Him and in a relationship there is communication.

God spoke to Adam, Abraham, Moses, Ananias and so many others in both the Old and New Testament. And He wants to talk to us too.

"My sheep listen to my voice; I know them and they follow me." John 10:27

I found out that God speaks in a multitude of ways. Just like we do. People don't just communicate verbally. There is our bodily language, that frown, that smile, allowing us to understand if people agree or disagree. So often words are not even needed, that lovely bouquet of flowers... or box of chocolates someone gives you, showing affection and care. There are also letters, emails, text messages, photos, pictures, video clips. So many ways of communicating.

Or just the presence of a loved one when you are distressed, when the world seems to crumble. It is a comforting peace you receive just because of their silent presence... or the hugs to let you know that you are loved.

God speaks to us in so many similar ways. Sometimes it is His amazing tangible presence overwhelming us with His perfect peace.

At other times, it is a Bible verse that seems to be particularly highlighted, almost as if it were written just for you.

Then there are those sudden unexpected thoughts flashing through your mind. You stop what you are doing and follow this gentle nudging of the Holy Spirit. And you find out that it was right to do so. Yes, you were meant to speak to that person. He/she needed that word of comfort.

Sometimes He speaks to you through someone who you may not even know, but what they say touches your spirit, encourages you, spurs you on. You know deep within you that God just spoke through the mouth of this person. It is a prophetic word, or a word of knowledge, of wisdom.

Then those rare but ever so precious times, when it is as if God speaks to you audibly. For me, it has happened only a handful of times. But those were key decisions in my life. A gentle whisper would not have been enough. I needed that almost loud audible voice.

Most of the time, however, it is just a sensing that this is the right thing to do, accompanied by a deep peace. That peace is a sure sign of His speaking. And, of course, the fact that it all lines up with the Bible.

It took me a while to discern the difference between God's voice and my own thoughts, my own desires. Sometimes I wondered. At such times, it is good to ask a mature fellow believer what they think. Do they confirm what you just heard? Godly counsel is valuable.

What if it is neither God's voice nor our own? What if it is the devil's voice, trying to tempt us, to make us fall? How can we discern the difference?

When God speaks there is always hope, even when He brings sin to the light. What He says is clear, it is not confusing. He may ask us to do something unpleasant, for instance, to forgive someone who has hurt us, but His words are accompanied by peace, followed by joy when we obey.

When the devil speaks, it may seem to line up with the Bible, but only partially. There is accusation, condemnation, bringing feelings of guilt, a hopelessness. There is no peace in our hearts.

With time, you learn to recognise God's voice. It becomes familiar. Until you just know that it is His voice. One way to learn is just to step out and obey when you hear His voice. Even if you are not sure, just step out and obey. Your confidence will grow, one step at a time.

There were times when I wondered, I doubted, I hesitated. Was that really God's voice? Sometimes the fear of looking foolish blocked me.

I also had to learn to deal with regrets. One day I shared my regrets with a wise woman, Joy. She listened quietly until I calmed down and then gave me these life-saving words: "Cordula, God is bigger than your mistakes!"

It was as if a lightning bolt had hit me. Of course! God wasn't walking around in circles, wringing his hands, wondering what to do just because I had blundered. He was not flustered. He would resort to another plan. He would sort out the mess I had made. He is able. He is bigger than our mistakes!

66

THE DOG AND THE CANDLE

On a lighter tone, here is an example of not hearing some-one else correctly.

I was chatting with my friend Maria. It was pretty cold in her part of the world right then. I asked how her dog was do-ing. Gideon is a beautiful German shepherd mix. He generally lives outside.

"He's fine. He sleeps in the garage."

"Is he OK there? Isn't it cold?" I was concerned. Tempera-tures were below freezing level.

Maria brushed my question aside. "Of course. He's got a candle."

"A candle?"

I envisioned her dog, lying in the cold garage staring at a lit candle.

"Isn't it dangerous? I mean, the candle could fall and set the garage aflame."

We were on Skype. The sound was not the best.

"What candle? What are you talking about?"

It turns out that Gideon had a kennel, not a candle.

And no, he didn't blow out his candle before going to sleep.

And he had a blanket in the kennel.

All was well.

Manufactured by Amazon.ca
Bolton, ON

19169882R00083